TV's Greatest GAME SHOWS™

Television's Favorite Game Shows From the 50's, 60's, & More!

by Tom DeMichael

Marshall Publishing & Promotions, Inc.
Barrington, Illinois

TV's Greatest GAME SHOWS™

Table of Contents

Preface

Television game shows of the 1950s and 1960s are extensions of the kinds of game shows that entertained radio listeners during the 1930s and 1940s (many of which were carry-overs from one medium to the other.) Before that, Americans entertained themselves with parlor games of *Charades* and pencil-and-paper games like *Tic-Tac-Toe* (both of which would play a substantial role in TV game shows.) Today, the line between game shows and reality programs is blurred and difficult to define.

For me, the line was always clear. As a Baby Boomer growing up in the 1960s, I recall shows like *Concentration, Video Village, What's My Line?* and *You Don't Say*. These shows *were* reality – people showed up on the screen of my folks' black and white Zenith every day and won money, prizes and – sometimes – the chance to return the next time to do it all over again.

Their ability to solve puzzles and answer questions intrigued me. Plus, they seemed to get everyone's attention, which is why I still like game shows today (in fact, I'm watching one right now as I write this.) I became pretty good at solving puzzles and answering questions. I'm the guy that everyone seems to call with that obscure sports or movie question. I'm the one that no one will play *Trivial Pursuit* with anymore. I work crossword puzzles with an ink pen. I'm the one that everyone wants to have on their *Charades* team. I'm the person that everyone says should be on *Jeopardy!* (it's not like I haven't tried.)

Bragging? I don't believe so, since – 1) they're just the facts and, 2) I never consciously made a decision to be the above-mentioned person. But I did consciously make a decision to be on *Who Wants to Be A Millionaire?* And, I made it.

Like millions of Americans, I was swept up in the *Millionaire* phenomenon in 2000. It was a show where it didn't matter how you looked or how perky your personality was – an appearance on *Millionaire* was predicated on a lot of luck and the ability to be quick and accurate in correctly answering questions. No TV producer or contestant coordinator screened you before you were selected. With luck, I made it to New York (pre-9/11) and taped an appearance. But, alas, I never made it to the "Hot Seat." Although I correctly arranged my "Fastest Finger" questions on the show, I was second to players who were actually milliseconds faster (as pointed out by my dad. Thanks, Pop.) No matter, it was a great – check that – an AMAZING experience and one I am very proud to have achieved.

So, I join the millions of people who have had their "15 minutes of fame" (actually 22 minutes, since commercials take up the other eight in a half-hour show.) And I still enjoy TV game shows – enough to write a book about them. I trust you will find your favorite included here. Many of mine are.

And that's my final answer.
Tom DeMichael
March, 2009

A note about how this book is organized - Game shows are alphabetical within each chapter heading, although they are not chronological in order. An index of games shows and people is found on page 218.

Let the Games Begin!

The Early Days of TV Game Shows

Let the Games Begin!

The Early Days of TV Game Shows

It should come as no surprise to note that many of television's first game shows were extensions of those that had originated on radio. Many broadcasting historians acknowledge that the first radio quiz show (referred to as an "audience participation program") was broadcast in October of 1936, as CBS offered *Professor Quiz*. Featuring the affable and highly intelligent Dr. Craig Earl, contestants would ask Earl the questions and, if they could stump him, they collected $25. The popularity of these quiz shows grew rapidly, with programs like *Doctor IQ, Pot O'Gold*, and the highly successful *Information, Please*. A 1940's program known as *Take It or Leave It* established the "$64 question" as an icon for an important challenge (later to become TV's *$64,000 Question*.)

Before World War II temporarily halted television's development, broadcast networks were hard-pressed to provide any semblance of a programming schedule. In Jeff Kisselhoff's marvelous book on TV history, *The Box*, CBS producer Gil Fates states that fifteen hours a week were tough to fill. Staffers talked about doing some sort of quiz show, coming up with the *CBS Television Quiz* in July

George Fenneman & Groucho Marx

of 1941 – making it network TV's very first game show. Fates hosted the one-hour weekly show that lasted for a year.

By the late 1940s, a mustachioed, cigar-smoking movie comedian named Groucho Marx had turned his rapier wit into the basis of a radio quiz show called *You Bet Your Life*. Marx would chat with contestants (getting huge laughs at their expense) then ask questions in exchange for prize money. With the advent of video, *You Bet Your Life* made an easy transition to the NBC television network in 1950. The popular quiz show would stay in the Top 20 of the Nielsen ratings for most of the 1950s.

***The Quiz Kids* Radio Show**

Similar successful shifts to TV followed for quiz shows like *Truth or Consequences*, which had started as a radio program in July of 1941. Where previous shows focused on knowledge and answering questions, creator Ralph Edwards had given *Truth or Consequences* a sense of humor, emphasizing stunts and antics for the contestants. Others making the move from radio to TV included *Winner Take All, Beat the Clock*, and *Quiz Kids*.

Television soon lead to programs of three distinct types: "Quiz shows" depended on questions and answers, knowledge and acumen. "Game shows" relied on daring and fearless contestants who participated in physical and (sometimes) athletic challenges. "Panel shows" brought celebrities and everyday people together, guessing who had a secret or what their line was. All three formats added up to popular entertainment in the early days of TV. The ratings of the 1950s often counted these shows as several of each year's Top 20 programs.

It was obvious that the best game shows were the ones with a simple premise. *What's My Line* merely asked: "What does that person do for a living?" *To Tell the Truth* basically picked two liars out of three people. *The Price Is Right* was just about the cost of an item. *Jeopardy!* gave the answer; the contestants had to give the question. Many game shows also relied on parlor games and other pastimes that the viewers already knew. *Pantomime Quiz, Stump the Stars* and *Win, Lose or Draw* based themselves on charades and other party guessing games. *Tic, Tac, Dough* and *Hollywood Squares* were simply large-scale versions of Tic – Tac – Toe without the paper. Card games like Blackjack and High-Low influenced *Twenty-One* and *Card Sharks*, respectively.

By the mid-1950s, game shows had the attention of the entire country. The *$64,000 Question* was the number one rated program of the 1955-1956 season. Other shows, like *Twenty-One* and *Dotto*, showed similar success. Unfortunately, producers of shows like these lost sight of their integrity and, in the pursuit of "entertainment," began to influence the shows' outcomes. It was called "controlling" and it was rampant among the quiz shows. Contestants with specific areas of knowledge were chosen, with questions in those categories routinely asked on the shows, and the result was week after week of consistent winning. Other producers were more direct – they supplied the questions and answers to the contestants they wanted to win. If ratings or show sponsors indicated the player had peaked, then they suddenly found

Twenty-One

themselves being asked legitimate questions – ones to which they just might not know the answers.

The final Golden Egg eaten by the goose who had laid it was *Twenty-One*. In 1956, a 29 year-old New York City college student named Herbert Stempel won nearly $50,000 on the show by following the coaching of show producer Dan Enright. With prior knowledge of the questions and answers, and a nerdy public image sculpted by Enright, Stempel was asked to dump his throne to a handsome instructor at Columbia University named Charles Van Doren. Even more galling to Stempel was that he was expected to take his dive by missing a question on one of his favorite films, "Marty." While Van Doren's sudden success landed him on the cover of *Time* magazine and a regular spot on NBC's *Today Show*, Stempel lost his winnings and appealed to Enright for a job. The producer, fearing the truth could come out, stalled Stempel by offering a panel show opportunity. When it failed to materialize, Stempel spilled his story to a local newspaper (who declined to print it.) But, when a stolen page of advance questions and answers from *Dotto* surfaced a year later, people began to take a look at quiz shows. Stempel's story was published and a Congressional committee was convened to investigate the inner workings of television quiz shows. While Van Doren had long contended he was above such shenanigans, his testimony before the committee in November of 1959 revealed the truth about his receiving advance assistance in his quiz show success that had won him nearly $140,000.

Dotto

The aftermath of the quiz show scandals was two-fold. First, game shows of all kinds disappeared from TV programming schedules, especially in prime time. Certainly, *Twenty-One, The $64,000 Question* and *Dotto* went off the air, while producers like Dan Enright were blacklisted for years. When game shows began to resurface in the 1960s, limits appeared on the amount of money a contestant could win and how many times they could win on one show. Secondly, the long-standing habit of sponsors holding control over all aspects of a program began to slowly deteriorate, leading to the demise of the sponsored program and an increase of individual commercials, or "spot" advertising in TV shows.

Even when game shows started to make a comeback, they weren't always on the mark. Jackie Gleason, ever-popular from his days as Ralph Kramden on the *Honeymooners*, took a shot at creating a game show for CBS in 1961. Called *You're In the Picture*, it featured four celebrity panelists who placed their heads through holes in a large picture.

You're In the Picture

Then they asked questions of Gleason to find out what the picture was. Critics ravaged the show. According to Gleason in a 1985 TV interview with Johnny Carson, "it laid…the biggest bomb in history." Over CBS's objections, Gleason went on the air the next week and apologized for the program. His half-hour apology turned out to be much more entertaining than the game show he had produced.

WACKY STUNTS & PLENTY OF ACTION

Wacky Stunts & Plenty of Action

American Gladiators (First series)

September 16, 1989 – September 13, 1996 (7 seasons)

Network:	Syndicated
Host(s):	Mike Adamle, Joe Theismann, Todd Christensen, Larry Csonka, Lisa Malosky, Danny Lee Clark
Creator(s):	Dan Carr, John Ferraro
Producer:	Trans World International, Four Point Entertainment, Samuel Goldwyn Television
Director:	Bob Levy

American Gladiators (Second series)

January 8, 2008 – August 4, 2008 (2 seasons)

Network:	NBC
Host(s):	Hulk Hogan, Laila Ali
Creator(s):	Dan Carr, John Ferraro
Producer:	MGM Television, Reveille Productions
Director:	J. Rupert Thompson

Everyday athletes pitted against muscle-bulging, lightning-reflexed opponents in a modern-day Coliseum – that's *American Gladiators* in a nutshell. Two male and two female contestants competed individually in tests of speed, strength, and endurance against imposing adversaries with names like Nitro, Zap, Gemini, Storm and Laser.

Hosted by former NFL players like Mike Adamle, Joe Theismann, Todd Christensen, and Larry Csonka, the tournament-style, 60-minute show offered many events for the contestants, including:

- Assault – As a Gladiator fired a gun shooting 100 mph tennis balls, the challenger scrambled across the multi-station course, using various weapons to hit a bulls-eye above the Gladiator.

- Joust – Perched atop small platforms, a contestant and Gladiator went at each other with padded jousting sticks (looking like Q-Tips on steroids.) The first to be knocked off onto the mat was the loser.

- Breakthrough and Conquer – Two-fisted action, as the contestant crossed ten yards against a Gladiator defender in an attempt to score like a football running back, then immediately into a wrestling ring to grapple with another Gladiator.

- Powerball – Both competitors vied to score by getting soccer balls into waist-high baskets, as multiple Gladiators bumped, thumped, and tackled them. One of the rougher, more physical games.

- The Wall – With only a few seconds head start, the contestants scrambled up a climbing wall, while Gladiators followed in hot pursuit. Grabbing an ankle or leg, they could pull the challenger off in defeat (although a safety harness kept broken bones to a minimum.)

- Hang Tough – Gladiator and contestant faced each other amid a maze of hanging rings. The contestant had to cross over, hand to hand, to the other side without being caught and knocked off by the Gladiator.

- The Eliminator – The final competition featured a harrowing obstacle course, as contestants sought to complete it in the shortest time. Starting with a climb up a down escalator, they moved into a rigorous hand-bicycle, followed with a run across a rolling log and a climb up a cargo net. At the top, the contestants took a quick trip down a zip line, crossed several hurdles and broke through a paper wall, where they might encounter a Gladiator intent on slowing them down.

American Gladiators originally taped at Universal Studios Hollywood for its first two seasons, then moved to the Gladiator Arena, specially-built at CBS Studios. It was a successful show, running for 139 episodes through 1996. Grand Championships earned winners cash prizes from $10,000 to $30,000 (rising as the show gained popularity) and new cars.

***American Gladiators* - 1989**

Talk of a revival began in 2007 and the revised *American Gladiators* appeared on NBC in January of 2008. Now hosted by actor and pro wrestler Hulk Hogan and pro boxer Laila Ali (daughter of the ex-champ Muhammad Ali,) the program alternated between 60 minutes for the preliminary competitions, 90 minutes for the semi-finals, and two hours for the finals. Now being shot at Sony Pictures Studios, the show featured some new events, as well as upgraded versions from the original series. A

American Gladiators - 2008

pool of water was added to the Joust, Hang Tough, and to the Eliminator, which also featured fire for contestants to swim under.

Winners of the Grand Championship earned $100,000, a new car, and the role of Gladiator in the upcoming season of *American Gladiators*.

<u>Beat the Clock</u> (First series)

March 23, 1950 – January 30, 1961 (11 seasons)

Network:	CBS (1950 – 1958) ABC (1958 – 1961)
Host(s):	Clayton "Bud" Collier
Creator(s):	Mark Goodson, Bill Todman
Producer:	Goodson – Todman Productions
Director(s):	Paul Alter, Lloyd Gross, Franklin Heller, Byron Paul, Jerome Schnur, Ira Skutch.

<u>Beat the Clock</u> (Second series)

September 15, 1969 – September 20, 1974 (5 seasons)

Network:	Syndicated
Host(s):	Jack Narz, Gene Wood
Creator(s):	Mark Goodson, Bill Todman
Producer(s):	Mark Goodson, Robert Kline, Bill Todman
Director:	Paul Alter, Trevor Evans, Ira Skutch

<u>Beat the Clock</u> (Third series)

September 17, 1979 – February 1, 1980 (1 season)

Network:	CBS
Host(s):	Monty Hall
Creator(s):	Mark Goodson, Bill Todman
Producer(s):	Mark Goodson, Bill Todman, Frank Wayne
Director:	Paul Alter

Beat the Clock (Fourth series)

September 5, 2002 – September 4, 2003 (1 season)

Network:	PAX
Host(s):	Gary Kroeger
Creator(s):	Mark Goodson, Bill Todman
Producer(s):	Mark Maxwell-Smith
Director:	NA

Following a successful 1949 season as a radio show for CBS, *Beat the Clock* premiered on TV in March of 1950. It would become a long-sustaining program with generations of fans.

Hosted by Clayton "Bud" Collier (who had voiced the role of Superman on radio in the 1940s,) *Beat the Clock* pitted contestants in silly stunts of skill against a ticking clock. The goal was to accomplish their game before the seconds had ticked away. There was never a shortage of blindfolds, cream pies, or paper cups, as Collier became known as "America's number one clockwatcher." The show was sponsored for the first six years by Sylvania, an electronics manufacturer, followed by Hazel Bishop, a cosmetics company that provided financial support for the next year.

Beat the Clock

The show's contestants were pulled from the studio audience, many of whom were married or engaged couples. Many of the stunts resembled

Beat the Clock

those that might have been played at a child's birthday party, as contestants tried to carry, catch, or place items in a limited amount of time. Collier would explain the task to be completed, usually stopping to note "the catch." For example, the contestant was to carry a balloon from one spot to another – BUT, of course, they couldn't use their hands.

One illustration of a *Beat the Clock* stunt involved a husband lying on his back while his wife rolled little wooden hoops down a trough. Holding a cylindrical oatmeal container in each hand, the husband had to catch five of the hoops between the containers – all within 50 seconds (he did it in about 20 seconds.) Another required a wife to place four coffee cups atop each other on the floor within 55 seconds - while whirling around seated on a four-wheeled dolly that her husband pulled in a large circle with a rope. Winners of contests like these would gain cash prizes, plus moving on to more challenging and rewarding bonus rounds.

After an eight year layoff, *Beat the Clock* returned to syndicated TV in 1969, now with host Jack Narz (and later, Gene Wood.) This version featured two couples who competed for prizes, along with occasional guest celebrities who performed solo stunts. Using many of the same creative team from the first series, the show was popular for another five years.

CBS revisited *Beat the Clock* for the 1979 season, this time featuring Monty Hall as host, along with three terry-cloth clad female assistants. Still following the basic premise of the original show, this version featured stunts like a wife placing mints on her husband's forehead, which he tried to get into his mouth without using his hands. Slated for 45 seconds, the hubby succeeded with ten seconds to spare.

***Beat the Clock* - 2002**

Beat the Clock made it to the 21st Century, more than 50 years after it first aired. The Christian network, PAX, brought former *Saturday Night Live* skit player Gary Kroeger to host the show along with model Julielinh Parker. Three teams competed for prizes in one season on TV.

Card Sharks (First series)

April 24, 1978 – October 23, 1981 (3 seasons)

Network:	NBC
Host(s):	Jim Perry
Creator(s):	Mark Goodson, Bill Todman
Producer:	Goodson – Todman Productions
Director(s):	Marc Breslow

Card Sharks (Second series)

January 6, 1986 – March 30, 1989 (3 seasons)

Network:	CBS (also syndicated 1986 -1987)
Host(s):	Bob Eubanks, Bill Rafferty
Creator(s):	Mark Goodson, Bill Todman
Producer:	Goodson – Todman Productions
Director(s):	Marc Breslow

Card Sharks (Third series)

September 17, 2001 – December 14, 2001 (1 season)

Network:	Syndicated
Host(s):	Pat Bullard
Creator(s):	Mark Goodson, Bill Todman
Producer:	Goodson – Todman Productions
Director(s):	R. Brian DiPirro

Jim Perry

Another game show from the stable of Goodson and Todman, *Card Sharks* basically featured two contestants in a game of five-card High-Low. The one who came closest to a survey question was given first shot at playing High-Low, using playing cards the size of movie posters. The winner of this game moved on to "The Money Game," where cards in a pyramid-based progression won the player more money. In one example of maximum betting, a woman started with $200 and, betting the entire amount every time, beat "The Money Game" in seven card turns with nearly $30,000 – a very large amount of prize money for the late 1970s.

Card Sharks **- Bob Eubanks**

Canadian game show host Jim Perry was tapped to preside over the NBC version of *Card Sharks* for three seasons. When CBS picked the show up after a five-year hiatus, game show vet Bob Eubanks took the daytime reins. *Card Sharks* also went into syndication at the same time, hosted by Bill Rafferty. When *Card Sharks* was syndicated for a few months in 2001, Pat Bullard was the host.

Card Sharks **- Bill Rafferty**

Dollar A Second

September 20, 1953 – September 28, 1957 (4 seasons)

Network: DuMont (1954) NBC (1954, 1956 – 1957) ABC (1955 – 1956)

Host(s): Jan Murray

Creator(s): Jean-Pierre Blondeau

Producer(s): Mike Dutton, Jess Kimmel, Dave Brown, Bud Granoff

Director(s): Frank Bunetta, Dave Brown, Phil Levens, Martin Magner

Jan Murray

From the early days of television came *Dollar A Second*, based on a French radio game called "Cent Francs La Seconde" – 100 Francs A Second. Hosted by Borscht Belt comic Jan Murray, the show took married couples out from the studio audience and paid one dollar for every second they were on the show. They answered questions and performed humorous stunts, with the option of quitting at any time and taking their money home. As wives answered Murray's questions, a wrong answer usually resulted in a penalty for the husband. The risk of losing their money at any time was based on a random event occurring during the couple's time on stage. Supported by a timekeeper and staff announcer, *Dollar A Second* was sponsored by Mogen David wine.

One episode featured this challenge for a husband-wife team. While the husband sat on a slanted platform, slowly descending toward a pool of water, the wife frantically called random phone numbers – hoping to reach someone before her husband reached the water. After three calls, she connected and her mate was dry.

Joker's Wild (First & Second Series)

September 4, 1972 – June 13, 1975/September 1977 – September 1986 (16 seasons)

Network:	CBS (1972 – 1975) Syndicated (1977 – 1986)
Host(s):	Jack Barry, Bill Cullen
Creator(s):	Jack Barry, Dan Enright
Producer(s):	Justin Edgerton, Ron Greenberg
Director(s):	Richard Kline

Joker's Wild (Third Series)

September 10, 1990 – September 13, 1991 (1 season)

Network:	Syndicated
Host(s):	Pat Finn
Creator(s):	Jack Barry, Dan Enright
Producer(s):	Eric Warner
Director(s):	Richard Kline

Co-creator and host Jack Barry had lost favor in the public's eye following the quiz show scandal in the late 1950s. With a short stint in the business world and several years as a TV program packager, Barry found a new audience with *Joker's Wild* in 1972. The viewers of the 70s were part of a new generation who knew little of the previous shame of *Twenty-One*.

Two contestants played the game by pulling the over-sized handle of a slot machine. When the three tumblers stopped, they offered categories of questions for the players to answer for $50. If a joker came up on the screen, the money value doubled; two jokers increased the value to $200; three jokers won the game right then. A bonus game used the same device, but the screens were filled with cash amounts and "devil" cards that gave the player an immediate loss of accumulated cash and the bonus round.

Jack Barry

***Joker's Wild* tumblers**

Although the level of questions was not particularly difficult, some players made it seem so. One episode asked a contestant to name the only father and son team who became U.S. Presidents – the player wrongly responded "Eisenhower." A seemingly slam-dunk opportunity for her opponent fell apart when he wrongly responded "Roosevelt" (the correct answer was John Adams and John Quincy Adams.) The same duo was also unable to name gangster Clyde Barrow's female partner (Bonnie Parker,) lost aviator Amelia Earhart, Franklin Roosevelt's vice-president and successor (Harry Truman,) or Spanish explorer Hernando Cortes.

The episode was nearly as embarrassing as Barry's quiz show scandals.

Let's Make A Deal (First & Second Series)

December 30, 1963 – September 1977 (14 seasons)

Network:	NBC (1963 – 1968) ABC (1968 – 1976) Syndicated (1971 – 1977)
Host(s):	Monty Hall
Creator(s):	Monty Hall, Stefan Hatos
Producer(s):	Alan Gilbert
Director(s):	Joe Behar

Let's Make A Deal (Third Series)

September 22, 1980 – September 1981 (1 season)

Network:	Syndicated
Host(s):	Monty Hall
Creator(s):	Monty Hall, Stefan Hatos
Producer(s):	Ian MacLennan
Director(s):	Geoff Theobald

The All New Let's Make A Deal (Fourth Series)

September 17, 1984 – September 1986 (2 seasons)

Network:	Syndicated

Host(s): Monty Hall

Creator(s): Monty Hall, Stefan Hatos

Producer(s): Bob Synes, Alan Gilbert

Director(s): Joe Behar

<u>Let's Make A Deal</u> (Fifth Series)

July 9, 1990 – January 11, 1991 (1 season)

Network: Syndicated

Host(s): Bob Hilton, Monty Hall

Creator(s): Monty Hall, Stefan Hatos

Producer(s): Bruce Starin, Paul Pieratt

Director(s): Barry Glazer, Jim Maricione

<u>Let's Make A Deal</u> (Sixth Series)

March 4, 2003 – March 18, 2003 (1 season)

Network: NBC

Host(s): Billy Bush

Creator(s): Monty Hall, Stefan Hatos

Producer(s): Sharon Hall

Director(s): NA

Across the years, some TV game shows became part of the American lexicon – *Let's Make A Deal* was one of them. With a broadcast history that spanned forty years, the show provided some of the zaniest contestants ever seen on the tube.

Monty Hall with contestant

Hosted by Monty Hall for nearly the entire run, *Let's Make A Deal* offered game players the chance to trade simple items from home for unknown items that Monty offered. When one box might contain hundreds or thousands of dollars in cash, a curtain on the stage might conceal a live cow or announcer Jay Stewart dressed in toddler clothes atop a gigantic tricycle. All the while, contestants carried hand-made signs and wore outlandish and often clever costumes, hoping to get Hall's attention. Players came as Santas, doctors, brides, devils, convicts, farmers, and safari guides. As the contestants played pricing games and traded with Hall, they won modest prizes or cash or, if they lost in their deals, they would get "zonked" with useless trash. At the end of the episode, the biggest winners had the option of trading their gains for a chance at the "Big Deal of the Day," hidden behind one of three curtains on stage. The winning deals could offer vacation trips, cruises, appliances, even cars.

One typical episode featured a young woman dressed as Little Red Riding Hood who had gained $900 in cash in her dealing with Hall. She agonized over the chance to trade the cash for what was hidden behind a curtain on stage. When she pulled the trigger on the trade, she wound up with announcer Jay Stewart, dressed in oversized footie PJs, sitting in an enormous high chair.

An added feature in the 1970s gave winning contestants a chance at a "Super Deal," where they could risk everything they had won for up to another $20,000 in cash. In one instance, a mother and daughter teamed up to win luggage, a three-week Caribbean cruise, and cash totaling $10,000. Being a brave soul, mom traded it for door number three of the Super Deal. Instead of losing $10,000, the duo added $20,000 cash to their winnings – making a total of $30,000. It was a substantial prize amount for the 1970s (more than $160,000 in today's dollars.)

The doors of *Let's Make A Deal*

The popularity of *Let's Make A Deal* cannot be understated. It was a hit as both a daytime and primetime show and, when the program moved from NBC to ABC in 1968, it lead ABC to become the front-running network in daytime TV. The fact that it also appeared in six different series across five decades shows its appeal.

Hall would often fill time at the show's end by offering cash to audience members who could show common and not-so-common items. For example, he might offer $150 for a rat-tailed comb. In an infamous blunder in 1969, Hall noticed a young woman in the crowd holding a baby bottle with a rubber nipple. In all innocence, he suggested she could win $100 if she could show him another nipple.

Luckily, she didn't.

PDQ

August 30, 1965 – September 26, 1969 (4 seasons)

Network: Syndicated

Host(s): Dennis James

Creator(s): Merrill Heatter, Bob Quigley

Producer(s): Merrill Heatter, Bob Quigley

Director(s): Larry White, Jerome Shaw

PDQ was hosted by the master of game show emcees, Dennis James. The game's title referred to "Please Draw Quickly," which will be explained below.

Dennis James

Two teams of two contestants – two celebrities against a celebrity and an audience member – tried to guess words or phrases based on clues using plastic letters (which the players had to "please draw quickly" from a pile of letters.) Starting with abbreviations, players would add letters to a large marquee, while the other contestant was sealed in a soundproof booth (perhaps left over from the quiz show scandals.)

For example, one player might hang "MNT" on the wall, adding "I, E, G" etc., in an effort to get the partner to correctly guess "Minuet in G" before time was up. Then the other team would have a shot at the same phrase. Each round was won by the team who used the least number of letters. The winning contestant progressed to a "Bonus Round," where he or she had sixty seconds to decipher as many words as possible from three-letter clues – for example, "horse" from "hrs." Each word won the contestant cash – a good player could come away with as much as $500 in a bonus round. By comparison, the median U.S. family income at that time was approximately $150 a week. Like many game shows of the day, *PDQ* gave contestants the chance to win a month's salary in just a few minutes.

***PDQ* sound proof booths**

One episode of *PDQ* showed that game shows were capable of making mistakes – a clue in the Bonus Round offered "BDR" for "Board." It should have been "BRD."

A producer had to be pretty darn quick to catch errors like those.

Press Your Luck

September 19, 1983 – September 26, 1986 (3 seasons)

Network: CBS

Host(s): Peter Tomarken

Creator(s): Bill Carruthers, Jan McCormack

Producer(s): Bill Mitchell

Director(s): Bill Carruthers

Whammy! The All-New Press Your Luck

April 15, 2002 – December 5, 2003 (2 seasons)

Network: Game Show Network

Host(s): Todd Newton

Creator(s): Merrill Heatter, Bob Quigley

Producer(s): Michael Weinberg

Director(s): R. Brian DiPirro

Peter Tomarken

In the post-disco era of the early 1980s, *Press Your Luck* emerged as a loud, fast-action game show with big prizes for big risk-takers. Hosted by the handsome Peter Tomarken, the program quickly established itself in the rich history of television game shows.

The Big Board

Three contestants started the game by answering questions and accumulating "spins" to be used in the next two rounds. Called the "Big Board," the next round featured a lit and animated board displaying eighteen frames containing an ever-changing assortment of cash, prizes, or "Whammys." A contestant would take their spin, yelling "Stop!" when they wished to halt the animated board. Whatever the highlighted frame contained would belong to the player. Cash and prizes piled up, but if they landed on a "Whammy," an animated character danced out and dropped the player's winnings to zero and they forfeited their turn. Part of the game's strategy involved the chance for a player to pass spins along to the next player – which they were forced to use, increasing the chance for a "Whammy."

The first "Big Board" round offered cash amounts from $100 to $1500; the second round increased to $500 up to $5000, with prizes like furniture, appliances, and trips worth up to $7000. Special frames offered a "Free Spin," "Double Your Money," and the very-desirable "Big Bucks," which held the highest amount available in that round.

Michael Larson

Many contestants came away with "Big Bucks," indeed, on *Press Your Luck.* Contestant Michael Larson came away with a record amount of game show winnings in 1984, earning more than $110,000 – based on a little pre-show preparation. Using a VCR and the pause mode, Larson determined that the "random" sequence of the "Big Board" wasn't so random. He identified five definite patterns that repeated continuously and, armed with this knowledge, headed for Hollywood. Once on the show, he ravaged the "Big Board," at one point running an unbelievable forty spins without hitting a "Whammy" or using any of his saved spins. When it was all over, Larson had amassed $110, 237 in cash and prizes. The producers knew something was amiss, but couldn't prove anything and Larson received his winnings. But, they had learned a valuable lesson and designed a truly random sequence board to avoid a reoccurrence of Larson's feat.

Press Your Luck was reintroduced through the Game Show Network in 2002, as *Whammy! The All-New Press Your Luck*, with new computerized graphics and "Whammys" as well. But Michael Larson, who had lost all his winnings since the 1984 show, wasn't around to see the revival – he died of throat cancer in 1999.

Remote Control

December 7, 1987 – December 13, 1991 (5 seasons)

Network: MTV, Syndicated (1989 – 1990)

Host(s): Ken Ober

Creator(s): Joe Davola, Michael Dugan

Producer(s): Doug Herzog

Director(s): Dana Calderwood, Scott Fishman, Milton Lage

Just like MTV, the cable network that spawned it, *Remote Control* was edgy, brash and fast-paced. But deep-down, it was a quiz show that allowed contestants to answer questions and win prizes – just like the other TV game shows.

Ken Ober

The show was hosted by comic actor Ken Ober and supported by announcer (and future *Saturday Night Live* member) Colin Quinn, as well as hostesses Marisol Massey, Kari Wuhrer, Alicia Coppola, and Susan Ashley. *Remote Control* was goofy and irreverent, silly and campy – a show that never took itself seriously. Three young contestants were seat-belted into leather recliner chairs, set in the surreally-decorated "basement" of host Ober. Holding TV remote control units, they chose "channels" on a mock television, giving them

Colin Quinn

The *Remote Control* set

categories for music, TV, and pop culture questions. Various point values were given for correct answers.

Obviously, it was "anything goes" on *Remote Control*. There was always the possibility of being pelted by peanut butter and marshmallow sandwiches from above or getting a visit from the corny-joke teller, "Mr. Baggy Pants." A popular feature was "Sing Along With Colin," where the off-key announcer tried to croon popular songs as contestants attempted to finish the lyrics. When contestants were defeated, they were usually removed from the show by being sent crashing – chair and all – through the back wall of the set. A thirty-second "Lightning Round" allowed two remaining players to square off head-to-head. Answering the most questions entitled the winner to advance to the bonus round. Reduced to a final player, he or she landed on an adjustable bed to identify nine music videos in thirty seconds. If they did, their reward was usually a brand new car.

Moving into the 90s, MTV changed their programming toward reality shows like *The Real World*, leaving behind creative game shows like *Remote Control*.

<u>Shop Til You Drop</u> (First series)

July 8, 1991 – May 27, 1994 (4 seasons)

Network: Lifetime

Host(s): Pat Finn

Creator(s): Scott Stone, David Stanley

Producer(s): Stephen Brown, Kathy Cotter

Director(s): Jeff Goldstein, Bob Loudin

<u>New Shop Til You Drop</u> (Second series)

June 3, 1996 – August 14, 1998 (2 seasons)

Network: Family Channel

Host(s): Pat Finn

Creator(s): Scott Stone, David Stanley

Producer(s): Derek Che, David Sittenfeld

Director(s): Jeff Goldstein, Bob Loudin

<u>Shop Til You Drop</u> (Third series)

April 3, 2000 – May 26, 2005 (5 seasons)

Network: PAX

Host(s): Pat Finn (2000 – 2002) JD Roberto

Creator(s): Scott Stone, David Stanley

Producer(s): Marty Rudoy

Director(s): Steve Grant

What did TVgame show fans get when producers took *The Price Is Right* and crossed it with *Beat the Clock*?

Shop 'Til You Drop.

Shop 'Til You Drop

Lifetime, the women-targeted cable channel, created the show in 1991 as part of their original programming. Two teams of two contestants squared off in stunts in the first two rounds, with the winners gaining points and a prize from one of the shops in the two-story "mall" set. They could choose from cameras, furniture, jewelry, sporting goods, fashions, and books, among other items.

The third round was "The Shopper's Challenge," where the teams had 90 seconds to answer questions in a "lightning round" fashion. Each correct answer gained points for the team and the one with the most at the end of the round was named the winner.

The winning team moved into the "Shop 'Til They Drop" bonus round, where six packages were opened one at a time. Each contained a prize and the team had the option of keeping it or running to one of the stores to exchange it – all in an effort to accumulate $2500 in prizes in 90 seconds. If they did, they kept their prizes and won a lavish vacation as well.

Shop 'Til You Drop moved to the Family Channel in 1996 for two seasons, then was revived on the PAX Channel in 2000. Host Pat Finn left in 2002 and, when JD Roberto replaced him in 2003, the show had changed its locale and format. The multi-store mall was now replaced by a warehouse-style store. The first two rounds asked the contestants questions, rather than requiring stunts. The final bonus round essentially remained the same.

Pat Finn

<u>Supermarket Sweep</u> (First series)

December 20, 1965 – July 14, 1967 (2 seasons)

Network: ABC

Host(s): Bill Malone

Creator(s): Al Howard

Producer(s): Jerome Schnur

Director(s): Peter Molnar, Lloyd Gross

<u>Supermarket Sweep</u> (Second series)

February 5, 1990 – May 26, 1995 (6 seasons)

Network: Lifetime

Host(s): David Ruprecht

Creator(s): Al Howard

Producer(s): Joel Stein

Director(s): Chris Darley

<u>Supermarket Sweep</u> (Third series)

April 3, 2000 – May 23, 2003 (4 seasons)

Network: PAX

Host(s): David Ruprecht

Creator(s): Al Howard

Producer(s): Joel Stein

Director(s):   Chris Darley

For many television viewers, it was a dream come true. Imagine running wild in a supermarket, loading baskets with groceries, meats, cheeses – just about anything found in the store. Producer Al Howard introduced the idea in 1965, staging *Supermarket Sweep* in Food Fair grocery stores on the East Coast with Bill Malone as host.

1965 Opening Scene

Three teams – usually husband and wife – started with one minute of "Sweep" time and added to it by being the closest in guessing prices of grocery items. Each correct answer added ten seconds to their "Sweep" time. The second round of the game involved sending one player from each team on a wild shopping spree, collecting as many groceries as possible in their respective time limits. At the end, each team's baskets were totaled and the winning team with the highest total returned the next day to accept the challenge of two teams.

Al Howard brought *Supermarket Sweep* back in 1990 as part of the Lifetime cable channel's original programming. Character actor David Ruprecht now hosted from a TV studio decorated like a grocery store, and the show had some new rules, as well. Contestants were limited to five of any one item, to prevent them from piling up hundreds of dollars of prime steaks or costly general merchandise items. They also had to replace any items knocked off from the shelves – or pay a $25 penalty. The new *Supermarket Sweep* also offered an exciting new final round called the 'Big Sweep." The team with the highest dollar total from the shopping spree had the chance to win $5000 in cash. Deciphering three clues throughout the store would lead the winning team to the big money.

Following a five-year hiatus, *Supermarket Sweep* returned in 2000, this time appearing on the PAX network and running until 2003.

David Ruprecht

Truth or Consequences (First series)

September 7, 1950 – May 31, 1951 (1 season)

Network: CBS (primetime)

Host(s): Ralph Edwards

Creator(s): Ralph Edwards

Producer(s): Ralph Edwards

Director(s): Phil Davis

Truth or Consequences (Second series)

May 18, 1954 – September 28, 1956 (3 seasons)

Network: NBC (primetime)

Host(s): Jack Bailey

Creator(s): Ralph Edwards

Producer(s): Ed Bailey

Director(s): Stuart Phelps

Truth or Consequences (Third series)

December 31, 1956 – September 24, 1965 (8 seasons)

Network: NBC (daytime)

Host(s): Bob Barker

Creator(s): Ralph Edwards

Producer(s): Ed Bailey

Director(s): Bob Lehman

Truth or Consequences (Fourth series)

December 13, 1957 – June 6, 1958 (1 season)

Network: NBC (primetime)

Host(s): Steve Dunne

Creator(s): Ralph Edwards

Producer(s): Ed Bailey, Bill Burch

Director(s): Stuart Phelps

Truth or Consequences (Fifth series)

September 19, 1966 – September, 1975 (9 seasons)

Network: Syndicated

Host(s): Bob Barker

Creator(s): Ralph Edwards

Producer(s): Ed Bailey

Director(s): Jack Scott, Bill Chestnut

Truth or Consequences (Sixth series)

September 19, 1977 – September, 1978 (1 season)

Network:	Syndicated
Host(s):	Bob Hilton
Creator(s):	Ralph Edwards
Producer(s):	George Vosburgh, Mark Smith
Director(s):	Richard Gottlieb

Truth or Consequences (Seventh series)

September 14, 1987 – February 26, 1988 (1 season)

Network:	Syndicated
Host(s):	Larry Anderson
Creator(s):	Ralph Edwards
Producer(s):	Ed Bailey, Bill Burch
Director(s):	Joseph Carolei

Truth or Consequences holds a position in game show history that no other show can claim. Originally a radio show started in 1940, *Truth or Consequences* was the first game show telecast on the very first day of commercial television operation in America. The program appeared on New York City's WNBT on July 1, 1941 – five months before the US entered World War II. It started its regular broadcast run in September of 1950 on CBS.

1960s Opening Scene

The premise of the show, created by Ralph Edwards (who was also the program's first host,) was a simple one. Contestants chosen from the audience were asked to answer silly questions – if they couldn't before the irritating "Beulah the Buzzer" sounded, they had to perform an embarrassing stunt as the consequence. As the phrase went, "You must tell the truth or pay the penalty."

Ralph Edwards

For example, one show from the mid-1960s pulled two gentlemen from the audience, where host Bob Barker asked a corny question. When they couldn't answer it, the duo was introduced to a unicycle-riding guest named Scott Anderson, who was going to teach the contestants how to ride a one-wheeled bike as their consequence. One contestant was given a standard unicycle. The other, to his shock and amazement, received an eight-foot tall cycle. The pro took the first gentleman on a piggy-back ride on the unicycle, making jokes about how heavy he was. Meanwhile, the second contestant was fumbling with his cycle, making it obvious that he would be going nowhere fast. While the audience roared with laughter, the contestant tried to mount the cycle, falling clumsily to the floor. On his second attempt, the rookie amazed everyone by quickly climbing atop the bike and pedaling around the studio, coming to a stop in the back – eyes popping with fear. At that point, Barker let everyone in on the secret – Anderson and his remarkable prodigy were actually the famous unicyclists, the Valenti Brothers. They then entertained the audience with some exciting coordinated action. The other unknowing contestant won two pairs of slacks for his efforts.

Bob Barker

Barker hosted *Truth or Consequences* for seventeen seasons, leaving when the show closed in 1975. Back in syndication in1977, it lasted only one season. The show was brought back once again in 1987, with actor and magician Larry Anderson hosting the fun – which lasted for only six months before being cancelled.

Video Village

July 1, 1960 – June 16, 1962 (3 seasons)

Network: CBS (primetime, daytime, Saturday mornings)

Host(s): Jack Narz, Monty Hall

Creator(s): Bob Quigley

Producer(s): Bob Quigley

Director(s): Jerome Shaw

Shenanigans

September 26, 1964 – December 18, 1965 (2 seasons)

Network: ABC (Saturday mornings)

Host(s): Stubby Kaye

Creator(s): Bob Quigley

Producer(s): Merrill Heatter, Bob Quigley

Director(s): Hal Cooper, Stuart Phelps

It was one of the most unique game shows ever on TV, but one of the most obvious as well. Why not produce a game show based on a giant-sized board game layout? It was the perfect tie-in for a Milton Bradley board game, as well.

Two players acted as living "game pieces," moving along the three rows (called "streets") of actions and prizes, as their partners turned an

Milton Bradley board game

oversized dice cage to determine their turns. Starting on "Money Street," contestants could win a free turn or go to jail – a phone booth-sized cage on the set. Turning onto "Bridge Street," players could win cash or land on a space that took them across the bridge to "the Magic Mile." Once there, players visited various shops on their way to the finish line. Directing all the action was the host (known as "the Mayor") – with duties performed by Jack Narz and, finishing the series, Monty Hall. The show's announcer, Kenny Williams, was called "the Town Crier."

Stubby Kaye

A Saturday morning kids' version, called *Video Village Junior*, hit the air for one season in 1961. In 1964, ABC offered a kids' game show called *Shenanigans*, which was essentially the same as *Video Village Junior*. Stubby Kaye, Marlon Brando's co-star in the film version of *Guys and Dolls,* hosted the show for two seasons. Appropriately, the program was sponsored by Milton Bradley.

Wheel of Fortune (Network)

January 6, 1975 – September 20, 1991 (17 seasons)

Network:	NBC (daytime) CBS (daytime 1989 - 1991)
Host(s):	Chuck Woolery, Pat Sajak, Rolf Benirschke, Bob Goen
Letter-Turner(s):	Susan Stafford (1975 – 1982) Vanna White (1982 – 1991)
Creator(s):	Merv Griffin
Producer(s):	John Rhinehart, Nancy Jones, Harry Friedman
Director(s):	Jeff Goldstein, Dick Carson

Wheel of Fortune (Syndicated)

September 19, 1983 - Present

Network:	Syndication
Host(s):	Pat Sajak
Letter-Turner(s):	Vanna White
Creator(s):	Merv Griffin
Producer(s):	John Rhinehart, Nancy Jones, Harry Friedman
Director(s):	Dick Carson, Mark Corwin

Regarded as one of the giants in the history of TV game shows, *Wheel of Fortune* was based on one of the oldest and simplest of "rainy-day games"

– Hangman. Created in 1975 by Merv Griffin, *Wheel of Fortune* has lasted, on network and then syndication, for more than thirty years.

Susan Stafford & Chuck Woolery

Griffin's basic premise was to allow three contestants to solve a word or phrase puzzle, taking turns at spinning a huge wheel that provided money values – as well as bankruptcy and "Lose a Turn" pitfalls. Like Hangman, each turn gave a player a chance to guess a consonant – or buy a vowel – that might be in the featured puzzle. A player could guess the answer at any time, usually when enough letters had been revealed. The winner could take the accumulated prize money (although not actual cash) and "buy" prizes from various showrooms in the studio. The rules were changed in 1987 by dumping the prize shopping and replacing the winnings with real cash – it quickened the game.

Game show staple Chuck Woolery was the first host for the network daytime version until 1981, when Pat Sajak took over. Sajak left in 1989 (while staying with the syndicated version) and ex-NFL kicker Rolf Benirschke played host for one season. Bob Goen finished the daytime series through 1991. The all-important "letter-turner" role was

Vanna White, Pat Sajak, & the Wheel

originally held by Susan Stafford, who left in 1982. Replacing her was perky Vanna White, who flipped the rest of the daytime, as well as syndicated, puzzles.

While the daytime version had a solid run, the popularity of the show rose with the syndicated program. The on-air chemistry of Sajak and White appealed to viewers, as did the wild and enthusiastic players. Like many successful TV game shows, *Wheel of Fortune* allowed viewers to play along, proving they were as good as the people on the tube. In some cases, contestants made that all too easy.

In one instance, a contestant had (with some difficulty) solved the puzzle as "A Roman God Or The Planet Nearest The Sun." She did, however, blow a $3000 bonus by completing the puzzle with an answer of "Pluto." Another episode saw a contestant try to solve the following puzzle: "A _latter _f S_ _ _ l _ n _ Stea _ Fa _ _ tas" by responding, "A platter of steaming hot fajitas" (the answer was actually "A Platter of Sizzling Steak Fajitas.") A third example of tough gaming saw a player lose more than $33,000 by solving the following puzzle: "Glea_ing White Sand Beach," answering, "Gleaming White Sand BeachES!"

Merv Griffin probably never imagined such amazing answers.

CELEBRITIES of all sorts

Celebrities of All Sorts

<u>Can You Top This?</u> (First series)

October 3, 1950 – March 26, 1951 (1 season)

Network: ABC

Host(s): Ward Wilson

Joke-Teller(s): "Senator" Edward Ford

Creator(s): "Senator" Edward Ford

Producer(s): "Senator" Edward Ford

Director(s): Marshall Diskin, Roger Bower

<u>Can You Top This?</u> (Second series)

January 26, 1970 – September 1970 (1 season)

Network: Syndicated

Host(s): Wink Martindale

Joke-Teller(s): Dick Gautier, Richard Dawson

Creator(s): "Senator" Edward Ford

Producer(s): Sheldon Brosky, Perry Cross

Director(s): Martin Kane

Newspaper ad for radio's *Can You Top This?*

Following a successful run on radio, *Can You Top This?* premiered on the fledgling ABC television network in October of 1950. Originally created by vaudeville comedian "Senator" Edward Ford, the show featured jokes sent in by viewers that were told by Ford. A "laugh-meter" measured the response from the studio audience, establishing a score that a panel of star comedians tried to beat.

Can You Top This? ran for only one season in 1950, but was revived for syndication in 1970. Hosted by Wink Martindale, the new show offered Dick Gautier and Richard Dawson (pre-*Match Game* and *Family Feud*) as the joke tellers. Some of comedy's biggest names appeared as celebrity panelists: Danny Thomas, Morey Amsterdam, Jack Carter, Milton Berle and more.

<u>Hollywood Squares</u> (First series)

October 16, 1966 – June 20, 1980 (14 seasons)

Network: NBC

Host(s): Peter Marshall

Creator(s): Merrill Heatter, Bob Quigley

Producer(s): Les Roberts, Bill Armstrong, Jay Redack, Art Alisi

Director(s): Jerome Shaw

<u>Hollywood Squares</u> (Second series)

November 1, 1971 – September 1981 (10 seasons)

Network: Syndicated

Host(s): Peter Marshall

Creator(s): Merrill Heatter, Bob Quigley

Producer(s): Les Roberts, Bill Armstrong, Jay Redack, Art Alisi

Director(s): Jerome Shaw

<u>New Hollywood Squares</u> (Third series)

September 15, 1986 – September 8, 1989 (3 seasons)

Network: Syndicated

Host(s): John Davidson

Creator(s): Merrill Heatter, Bob Quigley

Producer(s): Harry Friedman, Scott Sternberg

Director(s): Steve Grant, Bob Loudin

<u>Hollywood Squares</u> (Fourth series)

September 14, 1998 – June 4, 2004 (5 seasons)

Network: Syndicated

Host(s): Tom Bergeron

Creator(s): Merrill Heatter, Bob Quigley

Producer(s): Claudia Cagan, Jay Redack

Director(s): Chris Darley

***Hollywood Squares* grid**

Another kids' game, another game show megahit – that was *Hollywood Squares*. Take two contestants and have them choose X's or O's from a gigantic, forty-foot tall, three-dimensional "Tic-Tac-Toe" board, filled with celebrities. The host asks a question of the chosen star and they give an answer that's true or false. The player has to decide whether the star is telling the truth or fibbing. Three across, down, or diagonally won the game for a player.

The success of *Hollywood Squares* fell squarely in the laps of the celebrities. Their ability to "sell" a made-up answer or sincerely answer a question truthfully was only surpassed by their ability to be funny. While host Peter Marshall tried to keep the inmates in check, they almost always got the last laugh. Tops among the mirth-makers were George Gobel, Jonathan Winters, Rose Marie, old-timer "Charlie Weaver" (actually Cliff Arquette,) and – resident of the coveted "center square" - Paul Lynde.

Peter Marshall (top center) & regulars

Many of the funny lines (called "zingers) revolved around topics that might have been a tad off-color – but funny WAS funny. For example:

- PETER MARSHALL: According to experts, is it ever okay to use a vacuum cleaner on your dog?

- PAUL LYNDE: I think it's better to walk him.

- PETER MARSHALL: When a couple have a baby, who is responsible for its sex?

- CHARLEY WEAVER: I'll lend him the car. The rest is up to him.

- PETER MARSHALL: True or false - a pea can last as long as 5,000 years.

- GEORGE GOBEL: Boy, it sure seems that way sometimes.

- PETER MARSHALL: What are "dual-purpose cattle" good for that other cattle aren't?

- PAUL LYNDE: They give milk...and cookies, but I don't recommend the cookies.

John Davidson

Peter Marshall stayed with the show until it finished its syndicated run in 1981. When it returned five years later, singer John Davidson was now behind the podium and Joan Rivers was permanently installed in the "center square." It ran in syndication for three years.

Hollywood Squares hit the screen once more in 1998, with Tom Bergeron hosting and Whoopi Goldberg spending several seasons in the "center square."

I've Got A Secret (First series)

June 19, 1952 – April 3, 1967 (15 seasons)

Network:	CBS
Host(s):	Garry Moore, Steve Allen
Creator(s):	Mark Goodson, Bill Todman
Producer(s):	Allan Sherman, Howard Merrill, Chester Feldman
Director(s):	Frank Satenstein, Clarence Schimmel, Paul Alter, Franklin Heller, Ira Skutch

I've Got A Secret (Second series)

September 11, 1972 – September 1973 (1 season)

Network:	Syndicated
Host(s):	Steve Allen
Creator(s):	Mark Goodson, Bill Todman
Producer(s):	Ira Skutch
Director(s):	Stuart Phelps, Marc Breslow

I've Got A Secret (Third series)

June 15, 1976 – July 6, 1976 (1 season)

Network:	CBS
Host(s):	Bill Cullen

Creator(s): Mark Goodson, Bill Todman

Producer(s): Chester Feldman

Director(s): Lloyd Gross

I've Got A Secret (Fourth series)

February 1, 2000 – 2001 (2 seasons)

Network: Oxygen

Host(s): Stephanie Miller

Creator(s): Mark Goodson, Bill Todman

Producer(s): Jeremy Hall, Dan Holton, Ross Kaiman, Jan Landis

Director(s): NA

I've Got A Secret (Fifth series)

April 17, 2006 – October 2006 (1 season)

Network: Game Show Network

Host(s): Bil Dwyer

Creator(s): Mark Goodson, Bill Todman

Producer(s): Terry Coyle, Melissa Mascari

Director(s): Robert George

Celebrities often appeared on TV by means of the "panel show" – a game show that featured a group of stars, combining their celebrity status with their ability to ask probing questions. *I've Got A Secret*, a long-running program of the genre, was simple enough – four panelists teamed up to determine a secret that the guest had shared with the host, as well as the studio and home audiences. The guest piled up cash for every stumped panelist and more if the entire panel failed to guess the secret. As Winston cigarettes was a long-standing sponsor of the show, winning guests also received a carton of smokes for their time.

Garry Moore (top) & panelists

In the beginning, Garry Moore was the soft-spoken host of *I've Got A Secret,* gently guiding the panel through the hits and misses of the show. Many times, celebrities showed up with their own secrets. Once, Harpo Marx was announced as the celebrity contestant. The real secret was that it was not Harpo, but brother Chico Marx in Harpo's costume. The panelists were stumped. Another episode introduced a guest as "Dr. X." Again, the panel was stymied to guess the identity of Philo Farnsworth, who had invented electronic television in 1922. Moore sent the genius on his way with $80 in cash, a carton of cigarettes, and the obvious observation that, "we'd all be out of work if it weren't for you."

I've Got A Secret lasted on CBS primetime from the Eisenhower administration into the thick of the Vietnam War. A syndicated version

Steve Allen

offered Steve Allen as host (who had also hosted during the first series) for one season in the early 1970s. Then, CBS brought the show back once more in the summer of 1976 for one month in prime time .

Women's cable network Oxygen revived the series in 2000 for two seasons, while the Game Show Network offered a season of *I've Got A Secret* in 2006. The not-so-secret secret to this version was that all four panelists were gay.

Masquerade Party (First series)

July 14, 1952 – September 23, 1960 (8 seasons)

Network:	NBC (1952, 1957, 1958-1959, 1960) CBS (1953, 1954, 1958, 1959) ABC (1954-1956)
Host(s):	Bud Collyer, Douglas Edwards, Peter Donald, Eddie Bracken, Robert Q. Lewis, Bert Parks
Creator(s):	Herb Wolf, Ed Wolf
Producer(s):	Herb Wolf, Ed Wolf, Allan Sherman, Alan Gilbert
Director(s):	Craig Allen, Lloyd Gross

Masquerade Party (Second series)

September 9, 1974 – September 1975 (1 season)

Network:	Syndicated
Host(s):	Richard Dawson
Creator(s):	Herb Wolf, Ed Wolf
Producer(s):	Alan Gilbert
Director(s):	Joe Behar

For many performers of the stage and screen (both large and small,) their tools of the trade include nose putty, greasepaint and crepe hair. These elements of stage makeup help transform the actor or actress into the characters they portray. One of TV's most popular game shows of the 1950s used stage makeup to create hours of fun. *Masquerade Party* featured a celebrity panel who tried to identify celebrity guests – disguised with heavy layers of latex and makeup. When the panel members were stumped, the guests won money for their favorite charities.

Host Peter Donald & Archie Moore

The great light-heavyweight boxing champ, Archie Moore, showed up one night as (pun intended) a ringmaster from a circus, just weeks from his exciting matchup with heavyweight champion Rocky Marciano. The Three Stooges – Moe, Larry, and Curly Joe – appeared on a January 1959 episode of the show. Dressed as the famous Gabor Sisters – Zsa Zsa, Eva, and Magda – they completely fooled the panel.

The real stars behind *Masquerade Party* were the makeup artists. Hollywood pros like George Fiala worked on the 1950s game show, also working on cult classics like *Santa Claus Conquers the Martians* and *The Brain That Wouldn't Die*. The 1974 version used the skills of Stan Winston, who would go on to win several Oscars for his makeup and visual effects work on movies like *Aliens, Terminator 2: Judgment Day*, and *Jurassic Park*.

Match Game (First series)

December 31, 1962 – September 26, 1969 (6 seasons)

Network:	NBC
Host(s):	Gene Rayburn
Creator(s):	Mark Goodson, Bill Todman
Producer(s):	Jean Kopelman
Director(s):	Jim Elson, Ira Skutch, Rodger Wolf, Mike Garguilo

Match Game (Second series)

July 2, 1973 – April 20, 1979 (6 seasons)

Network:	CBS (also syndicated September 8, 1975 – September, 1982)
Host(s):	Gene Rayburn
Creator(s):	Mark Goodson, Bill Todman
Producer(s):	Ira Skutch
Director(s):	Marc Breslow

Match Game (Third series)

July 16, 1990 – July 12, 1991 (1 season)

Network:	ABC
Host(s):	Ross Shafer

Creator(s): Mark Goodson, Bill Todman

Producer(s): Jonathan Goodson, Chester Feldman

Director(s): Marc Breslow

Match Game (Fourth series)

September 21, 1998 – September 10, 1999 (1 season)

Network: Syndicated

Host(s): Michael Burger

Creator(s): Mark Goodson, Bill Todman

Producer(s): Susan Flanagan, Jay Wolpert

Director(s): NA

For many TV fans, *Match Game* meant host Gene Rayburn chuckling at the bawdy comments of panelist Brett Somers or Charles Nelson Reilly in the mid-1970s. Few may recall that Rayburn had actually begun hosting the show in 1962 – and that the format of the show was somewhat different.

Gene Rayburn & celebrity captains

The first incarnation of *Match Game* featured two teams – a celebrity captain and two audience-chosen contestants. A question was asked and 25 points were awarded for a correct match between the celebrity and one of his or her teammates. If both teammates matched the captain, then 50 points were awarded. A total of 100 points was needed for a win, which netted the teammates $100. With a few changes, the show ran for six seasons, when NBC overhauled its daytime programming.

Rival CBS picked up the show in 1973 and the immediate changes were obvious. Six celebrities occupied a two-tiered stage, while two contestants vied for as many correct answers from all six panelists in two rounds of questions. The winner looked to earn as much as $5000 or $10000 by soliciting a fill-in-the-blank answer from one of three celebrities in the Audience Match, then going one-on-one with a panelist in the Bonus Round.

Match Game **celebrity panel - 1978**

The focus of the CBS version (also syndicated, starting in 1975) was the use of double-entendre questions and risqué answers, often featuring fictitious characters named "Dumb Dora" and "Old Man Periwinkle" – a far cry from the harmless queries in the 60s version. For example, a show from 1964 asked the contestants and guest captain Jayne Mansfield to choose "one word to describe (Russian Premier) Nikita Khrushchev" Jayne and one guest suggested "fat." By 1975, Rayburn was asking panelists and a contestant to fill in this blank: "The Big Bad Wolf said 'I just came from a house where this old lady had the biggest BLANKS I ever saw.'" With the answer being more than obvious, the entire panel (save for the dapper Richard Dawson) staged a comical walk-off. Eventually returning to their seats, three of the six celebrities matched the contestant's answer of "Boobs."

(L-R) Reilly, Somers, Rayburn, Dawson

The show left CBS in 1979, while syndicated versions continued until the fall of 1982. NBC picked up *Match Game* the following year, combining it with *Hollywood Squares* for a full-hour show. Rayburn continued as host of *Match Game*, while former Sha-Na-Na lead singer Jon Bauman led the *Hollywood Squares*. The show lasted one season, as did a 1990 revival of *Match Game* that featured Ross Shafer as host.

A syndicated one season shot was offered in 1998 – destined to go right down the BLANK without host Gene Rayburn and favorite guests Brett Somers, Charles Nelson Reilly, and Richard Dawson.

Name's the Same

December 5, 1951 – October 7, 1955 (4 seasons)

Network: ABC

Host(s): Robert Q. Lewis, Dennis James, Bob Elliott and Ray Goulding, Clifton Fadiman

Creator(s): Mark Goodson, Bill Todman

Producer(s): Peter Arnell

Director(s): Jerome Schnur, Herbert Hirshman

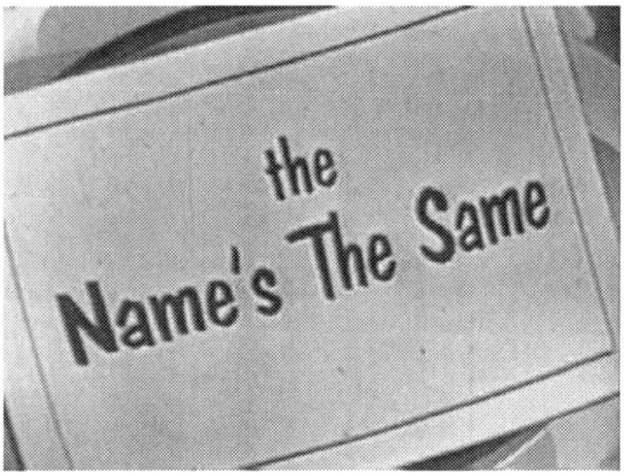

Opening credits

Once again, a panel of celebrities teamed up to ask questions of the show's guests. Why? The name of the guest was the same as a famous person (like "Abe Lincoln" or "Dean Martin") or a famous place (such as "Monty Carlo" or "Virginia Beach") or a thing (items like "Virginia Ham" or "Ginger Ale.") For every missed opportunity to name the guest, they received cash.

The show often presented a celebrity guest, who had a secret wish that the panel had to guess. Many times, the wish directly involved one of the panelists. For example, one show had a guest who shared his name with the comic western actor Gabby Hayes. Hayes then revealed (to the audience) his wish to see panelist and comic Arnold Stang wearing a grizzled beard like Hayes sported – a far cry from the milquetoast character that Stang often portrayed.

Facial hair became the center of attention on another show, as world-famous and eccentric artist Salvador Dali hoped to see "All men wear a

Salvador Dali & host Dennis James

mustache like mine." Known for his pointed and upswept handlebar, Dali was not able to stump the panel. He then drew a wild mustache directly onto the face of host Dennis James, who offered to have the famous artist sign his mug and immediately raise its "face value."

Password (First series)

October 2, 1961 – September 15, 1967 (6 seasons)

Network:	CBS (daytime & prime time)
Host(s):	Allen Ludden
Creator(s):	Mark Goodson, Bill Todman
Producer(s):	Frank Wayne
Director(s):	Lou Tedesco, Mike Garguilo

Password (Second series)

April 5, 1971 – June 27, 1975 (5 seasons)

Network:	ABC
Host(s):	Allen Ludden
Creator(s):	Mark Goodson, Bill Todman
Producer(s):	Howard Felsher
Director(s):	Stuart Phelps, Ira Skutch

Password Plus

January 8, 1979 – March 26, 1982 (4 seasons)

Network:	NBC
Host(s):	Allen Ludden, Bill Cullen, Tom Kennedy
Creator(s):	Mark Goodson, Bill Todman

Producer(s): Robert Sherman

Director(s): George Chodecker

Super Password

September 24, 1984 – March 24, 1989 (6 seasons)

Network: NBC

Host(s): Bert Convy

Creator(s): Mark Goodson, Bill Todman

Producer(s): Diane Janaver, Joe Neustein

Director(s): George Chodecker

Million Dollar Password

June 1, 2008 – (1 season)

Network: CBS

Host(s): Regis Philbin

Creator(s): Fremantle Media/Mark Goodson, Bill Todman

Producer(s): Vincent Rubino

Director(s): Mark Gentile

"The password is: longevity."

A game show that dates back to the early days of the Kennedy Administration, *Password* has moved into the 21st Century. In 2008, popular host Regis Philbin offered one-million dollars to contestants on (appropriately named) *Million Dollar Password*.

It was hardly the amount of money that Goodson and Todman had in mind when they took two contestants and paired them with two celebrities in 1961 to give and receive one-word clues in order to guess the "password." If one clue did the trick, the team received ten points – two clues to solve the riddle earned nine points, and so on, down to one point for ten clues. Improper clues, like more than one-word hints, earned the offender a loud "buzz" from an off-screen buzzer. A team score of 25 points led to the "Lightning Round," where one member had 60 seconds to get the partner to guess five words - $50 per correct answer, up to $250.

Some celebrity players were more adept at the game than others. Sixties talk show host Jack Parr got buzzed when he used "crew" as a clue for the password – which was "crew." Later on the same show, he repeated the gaff with "crank." *Petticoat Junction's* Bea Benedaret did the same with "smirk." Comedienne Phyllis Diller tried to get her partner to say "eats" by suggesting "masticates" – the partner didn't get it at all, responding with "fornicates."

Audiences loved *Password*, but CBS head Fred Silverman hated game shows, so he cancelled the show in 1967. Silverman replaced it with a soap opera, *Love Is A Many Splendored Thing*.

The ABC network picked up *Password* in 1971, moving it from New York City to Los Angeles, where it lasted until 1975. NBC took a shot at the show in 1979, renaming it *Password Plus* and upgrading the game by relating five guessed

Carol Burnett, host Allen Ludden, & Vicki Lawrence

Password Plus

passwords to a single password puzzle. For example, five rounds established clues like "roots," "branches," "chart," "ancestors," and "relatives," leading to one of the contestants correctly guessing "family tree" as the game's puzzle. The first two puzzles were worth $100 each, while subsequent puzzles were $200 each. The first team to reach $300 moved on to the bonus round, called "Alphabetics." The celebrity had sixty seconds to get the partner to guess ten words starting with ten consecutive letters of the alphabet (such as E – N or A – J.) When *Super Password* picked up in 1984 on NBC following a 2-year break, the rules were almost exactly like *Password Plus*.

Super Password

Allen Ludden hosted *Password* from the show's beginning in 1961 through the early 1980s in *Password Plus*. Felled by cancer and a stroke, Ludden was replaced by Bill Cullen and Tom Kennedy. When *Super Password* surfaced, Bert Convy hosted until the show closed in 1989.

The $10,000 Pyramid (First series)

March 26, 1973 – March 26, 1974 (1 season)

Network: CBS

Host(s): Dick Clark

Creator(s): Bob Stewart

Producer(s): Anne Marie Schmidt

Director(s): Mike Garguilo

The $10,000 Pyramid/The $20,000 Pyramid (January 19, 1976) (Second series)

May 6, 1974 – June 27, 1980 (6 seasons)

Network: ABC

Host(s): Dick Clark

Creator(s): Bob Stewart

Producer(s): Anne Marie Schmidt

Director(s): Mike Garguilo

The $25,000 Pyramid (Third series)

September 9, 1974 – September, 1979 (5 seasons)

Network: Syndicated

Host(s): Bill Cullen

Creator(s): Bob Stewart

Producer(s): Anne Marie Schmidt

Director(s): Mike Garguilo

The $50,000 Pyramid (Fourth series)

January 26, 1981 – September, 1981 (1 season)

Network: Syndicated

Host(s): Dick Clark

Creator(s): Bob Stewart

Producer(s): Anne Marie Schmidt, Sande Stewart

Director(s): Mike Garguilo

The New $25,000 Pyramid (Fifth series)

September 20, 1982 – July 2, 1988 (6 seasons)

Network: CBS

Host(s): Dick Clark

Creator(s): Bob Stewart

Producer(s): Anne Marie Schmidt, Sande Stewart, Francine Bergman, David Michaels

Director(s): Bruce Burmester, Dennis Rosenblatt

The $100,000 Pyramid (Sixth series)

September 9, 1985 – September 2, 1988 (3 seasons)

Network:	Syndicated
Host(s):	Dick Clark
Creator(s):	Bob Stewart
Producer(s):	Anne Marie Schmidt, Sande Stewart, Francine Bergman, David Michaels
Director(s):	Bruce Burmester, Dennis Rosenblatt

The $100,000 Pyramid (Seventh series)

January 7, 1991 – March 6, 1992 (2 seasons)

Network:	Syndicated
Host(s):	John Davidson
Creator(s):	Bob Stewart
Producer(s):	David Michaels, Erin Perry
Director(s):	Bruce Burmester

Pyramid (Eighth series)

September 16, 2002 – October 17, 2004 (2 seasons)

Network:	Syndicated
Host(s):	Donny Osmond

Creator(s): Bob Stewart

Producer(s): Tiffany Hoss

Director(s): Bob Loudin, Paul Nichols

Why mess with a proven formula?

Bob Stewart was a successful staff producer for the Goodman-Todson stable, creating *Password* in the early 1960's. By the end of the decade, Stewart had his own thriving production company. In 1973, he took the basic concept of pairing two contestants with two celebrities, who tried to elicit answers from their partners by giving clues to describe the word in question. Each correct answer gained the team a point. The first to reach 21 points went on to the bonus round. Sounds a lot like *Password*, right?

The game show was called *The $10,000 Pyramid*, which referred to the previously-noted bonus round. In the "Winner's Circle," the winning celebrity (usually) sat facing a large, six-paneled pyramid board. The contestant faced the celebrity, with no view of the board. The player had sixty seconds to identify all six topics from the board, based on clues given by the celebrity. For example, "an airplane, a cloud, a radio broadcast" might all be "things in the air."

Host Dick Clark

Dick Clark – "America's Oldest Teenager" – was selected to host the show, with a wide range of celebrities guesting on the show. Some of the best were David Letterman (long before his success as a late-night host,) Nipsey Russell, *M*A*S*H* star Loretta Swit, Bill Cullen (who hosted the syndicated nighttime *$25,000 Pyramid* show in the mid to late 70s,) Betty White,

Dick Cavett, and Vicki Lawrence, among others. Billy Crystal set the record in 1977 as the fastest "Winner's Circle" winner, earning his partner $10,000 in just 26 seconds.

The Winner's Circle

While inflation might have been to blame, it's more likely that the success of the show led to the increasing prize money across the years. Starting with $10,000 in 1973, the prize rose to $25,000 in the nighttime syndicated version in 1974. The daytime show was renamed as *The $20,000 Pyramid* in 1976, where it stayed until cancellation in 1980. Returning to syndication in 1981, it was now *The $50,000 Pyramid*, albeit for its one season on the air. The daytime CBS show was called *The NEW $25,000 Pyramid* in 1983, while the nighttime syndicated show hit the $100,000 mark in 1985. John Davidson's short run in the early 1990s also offered $100,000 in the "Winner's Circle," while the show hosted by Donny Osmond offered a graduated scale of $10,000, $25,000 and a shot at the $100,000 tournament.

Stump the Stars (First series)

September 17, 1962 – September 16, 1963 (1 season)

Network: CBS (primetime)

Host(s): Pat Harrington, Jr., Mike Stokey

Creator(s): Mike Stokey

Producer(s): Mike Stokey, John Hueners

Director(s): Bill Bennington

Stump the Stars (Second series)

February 24, 1964 – September 2, 1964 (1 season)

Network: Syndicated

Host(s): Mike Stokey

Creator(s): Mike Stokey

Producer(s): Mike Stokey, Joe Keane

Director(s): Paul Fuentes

Stump the Stars (Third series)

September 8, 1969 – September 25, 1970 (1 season)

Network: Syndicated

Host(s): Mike Stokey

Creator(s): Mike Stokey

Producer(s): Burt Wenland

Director(s): David Dunn

A televised parlor game sounds dull – unless it showcases Hollywood stars yelling and acting silly while playing charades. *Stump the Stars* was just that, having been born as *Pantomime Quiz* in the 1950s as it bounced back and forth between the CBS, NBC, ABC, and DuMont networks.

Opening graphic

Host Mike Stokey

Created (and mostly hosted) by Mike Stokey, *Stump the Stars* pitted two teams of four celebrities each - all decked out in tuxes and full evening wear - who acted out suggestions sent in by home viewers. If a viewer's submission was used, they received a cash prize.

The lineup of stars was never-ending – everyone from *Kids Say the Darnest Things*' Art Linkletter and the cast of the *Dick Van Dyke Show* to a pre-Lily Munster Yvonne DeCarlo and teenage werewolf Michael Landon. One particularly adept player was Ross Martin – sidekick Artemus Gordon to James West in CBS' *Wild Wild West* during the 1960s. Degreed in business, education (and a lawyer, as well!) Martin was a virtuoso violinist, spoke seven languages, and an accomplished actor, director, and makeup artist. A regular on *Stump the Stars*, he usually made quick work of the phrase being guessed.

The show was revived for one season in syndication in 1969. Ten years later, a clone called *Celebrity Charades* appeared for one season in syndication. A similar version appeared for one week in 2005 on the AMC cable channel.

<u>Tattletales</u> (First series)

February 18, 1974 – March 31, 1978 (5 seasons)

Network:	CBS (daytime) Syndicated (September 1977 – September 1978)
Host(s):	Bert Convy
Creator(s):	Mark Goodson, Bill Todman
Producer(s):	Ira Skutch, Paul Alter
Director(s):	Paul Alter

<u>Tattletales</u> (Second series)

January 18, 1982 – June 1, 1984 (3 seasons)

Network:	CBS (daytime)
Host(s):	Bert Convy
Creator(s):	Mark Goodson, Bill Todman
Producer(s):	Ira Skutch, Paul Alter
Director(s):	Paul Alter

Creators Mark Goodson and Bill Todman originally laid the groundwork for *Tattletales* when they syndicated a show called *He Said, She Said* in 1969. Former baseball catcher Joe Garagiola hosted celebrity couples who answered questions about their relationships. One partner answered the queries, while the other was sent to an isolation room. Answers were summarized into short phrases and the separated partners were reunited via

TV screens. When the clues were read, one of the TV-bound celebrities would ring in and relate a similar story. If the two incidents matched, points were awarded. Halfway through the show, husbands and wives traded places. The winning couple at the end of the show won a vacation for a couple from the studio audience. *He Said, She Said* lasted one season.

Host Bert Convy

Four years later, the show resurfaced on CBS as *Tattletales*, with Broadway star Bert Convy as host. The only real change in this version offered just three couples, each representing a third of the studio audience. Sometimes only matching yes or no questions, the winning team received cash that was split amongst their portion of the audience.

A sample episode might have found *M*A*S*H*'s Radar O'Reilly, Gary Burghoff and wife, squaring off against Miss Kitty from the long-running western *Gunsmoke*, Amanda Blake and husband, as well as game show host Gene Rayburn and wife. The men were asked, "Which one of you can read the other's mind better?" True to form, the Burghoffs matched, as Gary used his "radar" to read his wife's mind, while the other two couples failed to connect. The Burghoff section of the audience received a total of $1375, split many, many ways.

Ana Alicia & Lorenzo Lamas, Roxie Roker & Franklin Cover, Christopher Holder & Melody Thomas, host Bert Convy

<u>What's My Line</u> (First series)

February 2, 1950 – September 3, 1967 (18 seasons)

Network:	CBS (primetime)
Host(s):	John Charles Daly
Creator(s):	Mark Goodson, Bill Todman
Producer(s):	Gil Fates, Bob Bach
Director(s):	Paul Monroe, Franklin Heller, Frank Satenstein

<u>What's My Line</u> (Second series)

September 9, 1968 – September 1975 (7 seasons)

Network:	Syndicated
Host(s):	Wally Bruner, Larry Blyden
Creator(s):	Mark Goodson, Bill Todman
Producer(s):	Gil Fates
Director(s):	Lloyd Gross

Typical of the game shows that came out of New York City in the early days of TV, *What's My Line* featured four panelists and a host, all decked out in formalwear. They asked yes and no questions of their guests, searching for clues to what they did for a living – their "line" of work. Every "no" answer earned the guest five dollars, up to a total of $50.

Whatever the show was, it worked. It became the longest-running primetime game show in American television history, spanning eighteen seasons. As an example – when *What's My Line* first hit the air, the Korean War had yet to begin. When the show finished its run, America was deep into the Vietnam War.

Fred Allen, Arlene Francis, Dorothy Kilgallen, Bennett Cerf, & John Daly

Regular panelists on the show included actress Arlene Francis, comedian/composer Steve Allen (before his stint as host of the *Tonight Show*,) radio humorist Fred Allen, New York newspaper columnist Dorothy Kilgallen, and Random House book publisher Bennett Cerf. Their jobs were to determine if the kindly little old lady guest was really a lion tamer or if the young man seated to their left was actually the youngest licensed pilot in the country.

Following several of the regular guest segments, the "celebrity mystery guest" came on, with the panelists wearing blindfolds. The list of personalities read like a "Who's Who" of American history and pop culture – future U.S. presidents like Gerald Ford, Jimmy Carter and Ronald Reagan, Hall of Fame baseball players like Ty Cobb and Mickey Mantle, diverse musical composers from Rogers and Hammerstein to Frank Zappa, world-class artists like Salvador Dali, Norman Rockwell, and Walt Disney, award-winning performers like Marlon Brando, James Cagney, Bette Davis, and Jane Fonda. On the final primetime broadcast in 1967, it was only fitting that host John Charles Daly be the mystery guest.

When CBS decided that primetime was no place for game shows, Goodson and Todman brought *What's My Line* back as a five-time-a-week

Arlene Francis, Digby Wolfe, Suzy Knickerbocker, Bennett Cerf, Diana Ross and the Supremes

syndicated show, with Wally Bruner, later Larry Blyden, as host. The program ran for another seven seasons, until the fall of 1975.

In 2004, a live stage version of *What's My Line* appeared in Los Angeles, then moved to New York City (the place of its birth) in 2007.

Win, Lose or Draw (First series)

September 7, 1987 – September 1, 1989 (2 seasons)

Network: NBC

Host(s): Vicki Lawrence

Creator(s): Burt Reynolds, Bert Convy

Producer(s): Richard Kline

Director(s): Richard Kline

Win, Lose or Draw (Second series)

September 7, 1987 – August 30, 1990 (3 seasons)

Network: Syndicated

Host(s): Bert Convy, Robb Weller

Creator(s): Burt Reynolds, Bert Convy

Producer(s): Richard Kline

Director(s): Richard Kline

What do you call "charades" when they're drawn on paper?

Win, Lose or Draw.

Created by Burt Reynolds and Bert Convy, the show pitted two teams – men versus women – against each other. Two celebrities teamed with an audience guest to solve the puzzle within sixty seconds – one drew while the other two guessed. The winning team collected cash and could win more during the final bonus round, where a player had ninety seconds to convey as many single words as they could.

Host Vicki Lawrence

Vicki Lawrence hosted the NBC daytime version, while Bert Convy and later, Robb Weller handled the chore for the syndicated show. The rotund and hilarious Dom DeLuise, lovely Barbara Eden, perky Sally Struthers, pre-"West Wing" Martin Sheen, and manic Rip Taylor were just a few of the many celebrities that appeared on *Win, Lose or Draw.* As co-producer, Burt Reynolds often showed up to play, many times with then-wife Loni Anderson at his side. In fact, set designer John Mula based his concept on Reynolds' actual living room.

You Bet Your Life

October 5, 1950 – September 21, 1961 (11 seasons)

Network: NBC primetime

Host(s): Groucho Marx

Creator(s): John Guedel, Robert Dwan

Producer(s): John Guedel

Director(s): Robert Dwan, Bernie Smith

Groucho Marx & friend

A successful radio program for three years, *You Bet Your Life* was a poor excuse for a game show when it hit the NBC television airwaves in 1950. The show's achievements could only be due to one thing – its host. Perhaps one of the greatest American wits ever, Groucho Marx (leader of stage and movie stars, the Marx Brothers) used his sharp mind and sharper tongue to skewer contestants long before they ever had a question to answer, courtesy of announcer George Fenneman. Couples were brought out (male and female, but seldom married to each other) and proceeded to chat with Groucho. They were encouraged to "say the secret word" – a pre-established word that, if spoken, could earn them $100 – delivered by a mustachioed stuffed duck named Julius (which just happened to be Groucho's real first name) that dropped down into the frame. Pretty young women were a staple, giving Groucho the chance to bounce his eyebrows and tempt the censors with double-entendres.

Opening credits

One episode featured the enormous Swedish wrestler and B-horror movie actor Tor Johnson. Groucho took one look at the bald-headed giant and asked, "Who are you, Khrushchev?" (referring to Tor's resemblance to the Cold War Russian premier.) The wrestler corrected Marx, saying, "Tor Johnson." Groucho immediately responded, "You tore Johnson? Why? Did you get angry at him?" Marx proceeded to ask Johnson for his measurements, adding, "Personally, I'm not interested – but you may be an old boxcar the Union Pacific is looking for." Remarking on Johnson's 62-inch barrel chest, Groucho claimed, "We have the same measurements – your chest and my automobile." The comic continued, angering Johnson by claiming the city of Stockholm was in Japan, rather than Tor's home country of Sweden.

Groucho Marx & contestants

Other celebrities who crossed swords with Groucho included Harlan Sanders, a Southern gentleman who started the Kentucky Fried Chicken chain; the always-healthy fitness expert Jack LaLanne; a pre-celebrity housewife named Phyllis Diller; *Tarzan* movie star Johnny Weissmuller; heavyweight boxing champ Joe Louis; and U.S. Army General Omar Bradley.

Other attempts to replicate the success of Groucho Marx included a CBS version called *Tell It To Groucho* in 1962 (it tanked after four months,) a 1980 shot by comic Buddy Hackett (it held on for one season,) and a 1992

The one - the only - Groucho

attempt by Bill Cosby (who had received Groucho's encouragement to do the show nearly fifteen years earlier) – it also lasted one season.

After all, according to the opening intro of *You Bet Your Life* by George Fenneman, he was "the one – the ONLY – Groucho…"

<u>You Don't Say</u> (First series)

April 1, 1963 – September 26, 1969 (6 seasons)

Network: NBC

Host(s): Tom Kennedy

Creator(s): Ralph Andrews, Bill Yagemann

Producer(s): Ralph Andrews, Bill Yagemann, Dick McDonough

Director(s): Stuart Phelps, Bill Yagemann, Dick McDonough, Tom Belcher

<u>You Don't Say</u> (Second series)

January 7, 1964 – May 12, 1964 (1 season)

Network: NBC (primetime)

Host(s): Tom Kennedy

Creator(s): Ralph Andrews, Bill Yagemann

Producer(s): Ralph Andrews, Bill Yagemann, Dick McDonough

Director(s): Stuart Phelps, Bill Yagemann, Dick McDonough, Tom Belcher

<u>You Don't Say</u> (Third series)

July 7, 1975 – November 2, 1975 (1 season)

Network: ABC

Host(s): Tom Kennedy

Creator(s): Ralph Andrews, Bill Yagemann

Producer(s): Bill Carruthers, Gary Hunt

Director(s): Bill Carruthers

<u>You Don't Say</u> (Fourth series)

September 18, 1978 – March, 1979 (1 season)

Network: Syndicated

Host(s): Jim Peck

Creator(s): Ralph Andrews, Bill Yagemann

Producer(s): Bill Carruthers, Gary Hunt

Director(s): Bill Carruthers

If a viewer in the 1960s didn't double-check their channels, they might not know whether they were watching *You Don't Say* or *Password*. In fact, *Password* producers Mark Goodson and Bill Todman felt the same way – enough to sue the producers of *You Don't Say*. The settlement was simple – change the game so that it no longer was a mirror image of *Password*. So, the producers of *You Don't Say* moved host Tom Kennedy's podium from between the players (like *Password*'s) to one end of the set. Problem solved.

Host Tom Kennedy

Two teams – each with one celebrity and one audience member – earned points by giving clues to help their partner guess a famous name. For example, if "Lady Godiva" were the name, contestants might break that down into the following clues:

- To deliver an egg, a hen might…"Lay"
- A golfer places the ball on a…"Tee"
- Miners pan for shiny nuggets of…"Gold"
- In an Olympic event, a person jumping from a high platform would be a…"Diver"

Assembling those words correctly into "Lay+Tee+Gold+Diver" would earn the player one point – three points won the game and moved the winner to the bonus round.

The bonus board might offer a famous name such as patriot Patrick Henry. The board's first clue stated, "A poker player stands…" ("Pat") The second suggested, "On Halloween the children play Treat or…" ("Trick") The final clue offered that, "A house for female chickens could be called a…" ("Hennery") All three answers (Pat+Trick+Hennery) hopefully added up to "Patrick Henry" for the contestant. Guessing the name on the first clue earned $300; two clues meant $200; all three clues won $100.

Celebrity guests who appeared often followed a theme or featured primetime co-stars: Tina Cole and Don Grady from *My Three Sons*, Carolyn Jones and John Astin from *The Addams Family*, space travelers June Lockhart (*Lost in Space*) and Leonard Nimoy (*Star Trek.*)

Tom Kennedy returned to host the 1975 revival of the series, while Jim Peck handled the 1978 season. Kennedy's closing line from every show

Home version of *You Don't Say*

became sage advice for TV viewers everywhere – "It's not what you say that counts…It's what you DON'T say."

ANYTHING GOES

Anything Goes

Camouflage (First series)

January 9, 1961 – November 16, 1962 (2 seasons)

Network: ABC

Host(s): Don Morrow

Creator(s): Jerry Hamer

Producer(s): Gil Cates, Ron Greenberg

Director(s): Gil Cates

Camouflage (Second series)

February 4, 1980 – April 1980 (1 season)

Network: Syndicated

Host(s): Tom Campbell

Creator(s): Jerry Hamer

Producer(s): Steve Friedman, Mike Metzger

Director(s): John Dorsey

Camouflage was one of the more unique game shows to show up in the early 1960's. The object was to identify objects on a video screen that was covered with layers of random shapes. Two contestants answered questions, with each right answer removing a layer that would eventually reveal the object. When a player believed they could identify the object, they were challenged to do so with a large wand. The winner received a prize and the top winner of the day took the chance to find a hidden object within fifteen seconds, in the hope of winning a new car.

Don Morrow, longtime news announcer and commercial voiceover talent, acted as host for the first version, which ended after two seasons.

Milton Bradley board game of *Camouflage*

Nearly twenty years later, game show king Chuck Barris revived *Camouflage*, replacing the random squiggles with a cartoon drawing. But Barris, having spent more than fifteen years with successful game shows like *The Newlywed Game*, *The Dating Game*, and *The Gong Show*, had seemingly lost his golden touch and the show ran a mere thirteen weeks.

Concentration (First series)

August 25, 1958 – March 23, 1973 (14 seasons)

Network: NBC

Host(s): Hugh Downs, Bob Clayton, Ed McMahon

Creator(s): Buddy Piper

Producer(s): Jack Farren, Norman Blumenthal

Director(s): Van Fox, Ted Nathanson, Gertrude Rosenstein, Lynwood King

Concentration (Second series)

October 30, 1958 – November 20, 1958 (1 season)

Network: NBC primetime

Host(s): Jack Barry

Creator(s): Buddy Piper

Producer(s): Jack Farren

Director(s): Bob Taubman

Concentration (Third series)

April 24, 1961 – September 18, 1961 (1 season)

Network: NBC primetime

Host(s): Hugh Downs

Creator(s): Buddy Piper

Producer(s): Jack Farren

Director(s): Ted Nathanson

<u>Concentration</u> (Fourth series)

September 10, 1973 – September 8, 1978 (5 seasons)

Network: Syndicated

Host(s): Jack Narz

Creator(s): Buddy Piper

Producer(s): Howard Felsher, Buck D'Amore, Allen Koss

Director(s): Ira Skutch

<u>Classic Concentration</u> (Fifth series)

May 4, 1987 – September 20, 1991 (4 seasons)

Network: NBC

Host(s): Alex Trebek

Creator(s): Buddy Piper

Producer(s): Gabrielle Johnston

Director(s): Marc Breslow

What do they call the kind of puzzle that uses a bunch of drawings to represent syllables in a word or phrase?

A rebus, that's it.

Or, as game shows go, *Concentration*.

Hitting the air when Ike was in his second term as President, *Concentration* lasted for nearly twenty seasons on NBC and syndicated TV. Along with two shots at primetime in the late 50s and early 60s, the show returned in the late 1980s for another run of four seasons on NBC. In all, the show spanned the administrations of eight U.S. Presidents.

Like the kids' card game it copied, *Concentration* was simple – although a good memory was a plus. Two contestants faced a large grid with panels numbered 1 through 30. They would ask for a pair of numbers from the board – as the numbered panels were revealed, they showed various prizes, or commands to "Forfeit one gift," "Take one gift," or "Wild Card." When any two panels matched (or paired up with a Wild Card,) those panels would reveal a portion of the rebus. A player could guess the answer when enough of the puzzle had been exposed. If they were right, they won the game – if not, the turn went to the other player. Winners kept their prizes, plus cash.

The show originally belonged to producers Jack Barry and Dan Enright, but when the quiz show scandals forced them to dump all of their production holdings, the ownership went to NBC. Barry had hosted the first primetime version, while newsman Hugh Downs covered the daytime and second primetime shows. By

Hosts Bob Clayton, Hugh Downs, & announcer Art James

1969, Downs moved on and *Tonight Show* sidekick Ed McMahon hosted for a half-year. Show announcer Bob Clayton moved up to host until NBC ended the run in 1973. When the show was picked up by Goodson-Todman for syndication, it returned in the fall of 1973 with Jack Narz hosting.

Bob Clayton with rebus (WAA+SAW +RE+BUS = What's A Rebus?)

Brought back for NBC in 1987, the show was now called *Classic Concentration*, with Alex Trebek as host. The show was basically the same, with a few changes: the board (now a computer-generated image rather than mechanical) had 25 panels instead of 30, the "Forfeit one gift" panel was gone, and a new bonus round gave players a chance to win one of eight new cars.

But one doesn't mess with success, and the show was still a rebus game.

Dating Game (First series)

December 20, 1965 – July 6, 1973 (8 seasons)

Network:	ABC
Host(s):	Jim Lange
Creator(s):	Chuck Barris
Producer(s):	Walter Case, Larry Gottlieb, Steve Friedman, Mike Metzger
Director(s):	Bill Carruthers, John Dorsey

Dating Game (Second series)

October 6, 1966 – January 17, 1970 (4 seasons)

Network:	ABC (primetime)
Host(s):	Jim Lange
Creator(s):	Chuck Barris
Producer(s):	Walter Case, Larry Gottlieb, Steve Friedman, Mike Metzger
Director(s):	Bill Carruthers, John Dorsey

Dating Game (Third series)

September 10, 1973 – September 1974 (1 season)

Network:	Syndicated
Host(s):	Jim Lange

Creator(s): Chuck Barris

Producer(s): Walter Case, Larry Gottlieb, Steve Friedman, Mike Metzger

Director(s): Bill Carruthers, John Dorsey

Dating Game (Fourth series)

September 4, 1978 – September 1980 (3 seasons)

Network: Syndicated

Host(s): Jim Lange

Creator(s): Chuck Barris

Producer(s): Walter Case, Larry Gottlieb, Steve Friedman, Mike Metzger

Director(s): Bill Carruthers, John Dorsey

Dating Game (Fifth series)

September 16, 1986 – September 8, 1989 (4 seasons)

Network: Syndicated

Host(s): Elaine Joyce (The New Dating Game,) Jeff McGregor (The All-New Dating Game)

Creator(s): Chuck Barris

Producer(s): Walter Case, Bruce Starin

Director(s): John Dorsey, Linda Howard, Clay Jacobsen

<u>Dating Game</u> (Sixth series)

September 9, 1996 – June 9, 2000 (3 seasons)

Network: Syndicated

Host(s): Brad Sherwood, Chuck Woolery

Creator(s): Chuck Barris

Producer(s): Maureen Fitzpatrick, Joann Schoemann

Director(s): Paul Casey

It was the first of several golden eggs that would be laid by the self-proclaimed "Game Show King," Chuck Barris. *The Dating Game* was ultra-hip, with a set that yelled "SIXTIES!" And, like most of Barris' shows, it was full of double-entendres, sexy insinuations, and enough spicy talk to keep the network censors very busy.

Host Jim Lange with contestants

The premise of the show was simple enough. Three bachelors or bachelorettes sat on stools, hidden from their prospective date. He or she would ask prepared questions from cards – usually with a twinkle or wink in the eye. For example…

"Bachelor number one – one of my worst subjects is spelling, could you tell me – how do you spell relief?" Bachelor number one responded – "F-A-R-T."

"Bachelor number one – if I told you I was really ugly, but had strong bones and healthy teeth, would you still want to take me out?" Bachelor number one responded – "Sure – I have a nice farm I think I could use you on."

"Bachelor number two – I'm a dress designer. My fitting model is out and my deadline is drawing near. Would you be willing to get into my dress?" Bachelor number two responded – "Baby, I'd be willing to get into your dress, your pants, and anything else you got!"

Winners on the show received chaperoned trips around the world (which Barris claimed allowed him to carry out murderous hits as a clandestine CIA agent.)

Guest Paul Lynde (first chair)

Plenty of A-list (and B-list) celebrities made their way into the *Dating Game* chairs. A 14 –year-old Michael Jackson (unrecognizable by today's standard,) an eternally-effeminate Paul Lynde, the looney Rip Taylor, Paul Reubens (as Pee-Wee Herman,) handsome bachelors Tom Selleck and Burt Reynolds, and lovely ladies Farrah Fawcett, Sally Fields, and Suzanne Somers - all showed up on the *Dating Game* stage.

Body-builder, actor, and future California governor Arnold Schwarznegger appeared in 1973, leaving a memorable interplay with one of the eligible bachelorettes. After listing his Mr. Olympia-sized measurements, he asked, "What do we have in common?" Seemingly innocent, the young lady responded, "You get smaller as you go down." The audience burst into raucous laughter, catching the implication. The "Austrian Oak" quietly replied, "By the way – this is not true."

Perhaps the most memorable moment of each show was the close, where the winning couples joined host Jim Lange to throw a kiss toward the camera – usually themed. For example, winners going to Hawaii threw a "Hula Kiss," while a Christmastime show offered a "Yummy Yuletide Kiss."

For Chuck Barris, it was a delicious "Kiss of Success."

Family Feud (First series)

July 12, 1976 – June 14, 1985 (10 seasons)

Network: ABC

Host(s): Richard Dawson

Creator(s): Mark Goodson, Bill Todman

Producer(s): Howard Felsher

Director(s): Paul Alter

Family Feud (Second series)

September 19, 1977 – September, 1985 (8 seasons)

Network: Syndicated

Host(s): Richard Dawson

Creator(s): Mark Goodson, Bill Todman

Producer(s): Howard Felsher

Director(s): Paul Alter

Family Feud (Third series)

July 4, 1988 – September 10, 1993 (5 seasons)

Network: CBS

Host(s): Ray Combs

Creator(s): Mark Goodson, Bill Todman

Producer(s): Gabrielle Johnston

Director(s): Paul Alter, Marc Breslow, Andy Felsher

Family Feud (Fourth series)

September 19, 1988 – September, 1995 (7 seasons)

Network: Syndicated

Host(s): Ray Combs (1998 - 1994) Richard Dawson (1994 – 1995)

Creator(s): Mark Goodson, Bill Todman

Producer(s): Gabrielle Johnston

Director(s): Paul Alter, Marc Breslow, Andy Felsher

Family Feud (Fifth series)

September 20, 1999 -

Network: Syndicated

Host(s): Louie Anderson (1999 - 2002) Richard Karn (2002 – 2006) John O'Hurley (2006)

Creator(s): Mark Goodson, Bill Todman

Producer(s): Bob Boden

Director(s): Lenn Goodside, Ken Fuchs, Bruce Gowers

It is believed that success breeds success. If that's true, then *Family Feud* owes much to *The Match Game.* A lot of *Match Game's* sensation could be credited to the popularity of the dapper man who occupied the center seat of the lower tier – Richard Dawson. He was handsome, witty, and game players seemed to always call on Dawson for big money matches. This fact wasn't lost on producers Mark Goodson and Bill Todman, who crafted a new show built around the attractive personality of Richard Dawson.

Host Richard Dawson

Family Feud took two teams of family members and, one at a time, asked them to answer a question that had been posed to 100 people. For example, 100 people might have been asked, "Name a famous George" (as seen on the very first show in 1976.) If a player answered, "George Washington" and that was the number one answer, then he or she decided whether their team would play or pass to the other family (in the event the question seemed too hard.) The rest of the family was responsible to come up with other "famous Georges," such as "Burns," "Gobel," and "Jessel." If they couldn't, they earned a strike – three strikes and the control passed to the other family. If that family came up with a winning answer, they earned the points that had built up. If not, the other family won the points. Later rounds doubled and tripled the point values, with 200, 300, or 400 points being the finish line (the point levels changed during the show's run.)

The winning family moved into the "Fast Money" round, where two selected family members had to answer five questions – again, asked of 100 people – and try to total 200 points. If they did, they won the jackpot of thousands of dollars. If they came up short, they received five dollars for every point they had.

The key to the show was Richard Dawson. His debonair style and English accent allowed him to kiss almost every woman on the show. His quick wit seldom left him speechless, although there were times where he was caught short by dimwitted answers. In one "Fast Money" round, he asked, "During what month of pregnancy does a women start to look pregnant?", obviously looking for a numerical answer. When the lady answered, "September," Dawson was totally lost in fits of giggles for several minutes, unable to regain his composure. At one point, he fell to his knees, convulsing and shuddering with tears of laughter. Other crazy "Fast Money" questions and answers included:

Dawson with contestants on the set

DAWSON: Name one of the Three Bears.

ANSWER: Yogi. (What happened to Mama, Papa, and Baby Bear?)

DAWSON: Name an animal with three letters in its name.

ANSWER: Frog. (Apparently, dog and cat don't count.)

DAWSON: (Same question asked of the other family member.)

ANSWER: Alligator. (This one is even worse.)

DAWSON: Name a brand of gasoline.

ANSWER: Regular. (A brand usually means a company, like Shell or Mobil.)

DAWSON: (Same question asked of the other family member.)

ANSWER: Ethyl. (These are the same two goofs as the "three letters" question.)

DAWSON: Name something that comes with a summer storm.

ANSWER: Snow. (Maybe in Antarctica.)

DAWSON: Name something you might buy that could turn out to be phony.

ANSWER: A horse. (He said "Phony," not "Pony!")

DAWSON: Name something you squeeze.

ANSWER: Peanut butter. (Huh?)

Under the helm of Richard Dawson, *Family Feud* was, clearly, very entertaining. It remained that way up to its syndicated cancellation in 1985. Three years later, the entertainment continued when comedian Ray Combs took over a syndicated revival of the show. When ratings dropped in 1994, Combs was replaced by Dawson, who covered the final season.

Family Feud returned in 1999, hosted by Louis Anderson, Richard Karn, and John O'Hurley. All did a fine job, but couldn't match the style of awesome Dawson.

Gong Show (First series)

June 14, 1976 – July 21, 1978 (3 seasons)

Network: NBC

Host(s): Chuck Barris

Creator(s): Chuck Barris, Chris Bearde

Producer(s): Gene Banks

Director(s): John Dorsey, Terry Kyne

Gong Show (Second series)

September, 1976 – September, 1980 (4 seasons)

Network: Syndicated

Host(s): Chuck Barris

Creator(s): Chuck Barris, Chris Bearde

Producer(s): Gene Banks

Director(s): John Dorsey, Terry Kyne

Gong Show (Third series)

September 12, 1988 – September 15, 1989 (1 season)

Network: Syndicated

Host(s): Don Bleu

Creator(s): Chuck Barris, Chris Bearde

Producer(s): Rac A. Clark

Director(s): Jeff Margolis, Steven Santos

Gong Show with Dave Attell (Fourth series)

July 17, 2008 -

Network: Comedy Central

Host(s): Dave Attell

Creator(s): Chuck Barris, Chris Bearde

Producer(s): Jennifer Heftler, Matt Laesch

Director(s): Michael Dimich, Ethan T Berlin

Clever guy, that Chuck Barris. Instead of looking for the best talent, he went looking for the worst. Those that topped the bottom of the barrel found themselves on *The Gong Show*.

Three celebrity judges were forced to watch terrible acts until, unable to no longer bear it, they grabbed a mallet and stuck an enormous gong – mercifully ending the act. If the act could make it all the way through, the judges rated their performance on a scale from zero to ten. The top winner received a cash prize – in the unusual amount of $516.32.

Host Chuck Barris

Of course, not all of the *Gong Show* acts were bad – People like Paul Reubens (Pee-Wee Herman,) the band Oingo Boingo (with composer Danny Elfman,) "Annie's" Andrea McCardle, and vocal effects master Michael Winslow all appeared on the show.

But for the most part, the *Gong Show's* acts were pretty unbearable. For example…

- A bearded man spraying his head with whipped cream (with no musical accompaniment…)

- A Christ-like figure tied to a crucifix, singing, "Please Release Me – Let Me Go."

- A Dracula wannabe, hanging upside down while playing a banjo, until his tether broke and he crashed to the floor.

- An elderly man, clucking like a chicken to the tune of "In the Mood." When gonged by ex-baseball player Steve Garvey, someone yelled, "One more time!" prompting the man to once again start clucking. Gonged again, someone yells, "One more time!" and the old man is off to the races…Barris went to a commercial break with the guy still clucking away.

Barris with *Gong Show* act

- The famous "Popsicle Twins" – two young teen girls walked out on stage, sat down, and proceeded to eat orange popsicles in a most provocative manner (Barris explained that he often included acts that he knew would not make it past the censors, giving him a bargaining position for acts he really did want on the show. In this case, the censors didn't catch the infraction until it was already on the air.)

The Gong Show had its quasi-regulars as judges – most prominent was 50s torch singer (and lead instigator of offensive language) Jaye P. Morgan, comic Arte Johnson, actor Jamie Farr, plus others like David Letterman (before his late-night stints,) singer Dionne Warwick, and comedienne Phyllis Diller. And, the show also had regular bits and visitors, like the Unknown Comic (often censored,) Larry and His Magic…(a variety of musical instruments, which he never seemed to actually play,) and Father Ed, a man of the cloth who offered sage, albeit vulgar, advice to Barris.

Gene Patton

Another popular feature was Gene Gene the Dancing Machine – stagehand Gene Patton presented a foot-shuffling, tush-wiggling, fist-pumping display, while being pelted with hats, basketballs, mannequins, and other items from off-stage as the band played "One O'Clock Jump."

Chuck was never afraid of being the butt of jokes – his or anyone else's. While a tone-deaf singer wailed "Amazing Grace," Barris came on stage, supporting himself with crutches. Acting as if the song had healed his affliction, Chuck tossed aside the supports – and promptly fell on his face. Chuck himself got gonged when he performed "Take This Job and Shove It" as part of the "Hollywood Cowboys" players from music director Milton DeLugg's show band. The show was rife with corny jokes - "If Ella Fitzgerald married Darth Vader – she'd be Ella – Vader!" But Barris clearly knew what the show was all about, opening one show with "Welcome to the looney bin."

The amazing popularity of the *Gong Show* prompted the ill-advised production of *The Gong Show Movie* in 1980 (Barris still regrets the idea to this day.) But there was no doubt – *The Gong Show* was plenty of fun – on-stage, off-stage, and at home.

Name That Tune (First series)

July 6, 1953 – June 14, 1954 (1 season)

Network: NBC primetime

Host(s): Red Benson

Creator(s): Harry Salter

Producer(s): Harry Salter, Al Singer, Art Stark

Director(s): Perry Lafferty

Name That Tune (Second series)

September 2, 1954 – March 24, 1955 (1 season)

Network: CBS primetime

Host(s): Bill Cullen

Creator(s): Harry Salter

Producer(s): Harry Salter, Al Singer, Art Stark

Director(s): Perry Lafferty

Name That Tune (Third series)

September 27, 1955 – October 19, 1959 (5 seasons)

Network: CBS primetime

Host(s): George DeWitt

Creator(s): Harry Salter

Producer(s): Harry Salter, Al Singer, Art Stark

Director(s): Perry Lafferty

<u>Name That Tune</u> (Fourth series)

July 29, 1974 – January 3, 1975 (1 season)

Network: NBC

Host(s): Dennis James

Creator(s): Harry Salter

Producer(s): Ray Horl, John Rhinehart, Richard Gottlieb, Bianca Pino

Director(s): Terry Kyne, John Dorsey, Richard Gottlieb

<u>Name That Tune ($100,000 Name That Tune – September 1976)</u> (Fifth series)

September 9, 1974 – September 1981 (6 seasons)

Network: Syndicated

Host(s): Tom Kennedy

Creator(s): Harry Salter

Producer(s): Ray Horl, John Rhinehart, Richard Gottlieb, Bianca Pino

Director(s): Terry Kyne, John Dorsey, Richard Gottlieb

Name That Tune (Sixth series)

January 3, 1977 – June 10, 1977 (1 season)

Network: NBC

Host(s): Tom Kennedy

Creator(s): Harry Salter

Producer(s): Ray Horl, John Rhinehart, Richard Gottlieb, Bianca Pino

Director(s): Terry Kyne, John Dorsey, Richard Gottlieb

$100,000 Name That Tune (Seventh series)

September 10, 1984 – September 1985 (1 season)

Network: Syndicated

Host(s): Jim Lange

Creator(s): Harry Salter

Producer(s): Ray Horl, Peggy Touchstone

Director(s): Kip Walton

Name That Video (First series)

March 2001 – June 2001 (1 season)

Network: VH-1

Host(s): Karyn Bryant

Creator(s): Harry Salter

Producer(s): Ted Kenney

Director(s): Linda Mendoza

Music? Sure, everyone knows music – everyone can sing (so THEY say.) A game show that relied on popular music was sure to be a hit when it started on radio in 1952. It was. And, it was called *Name That Tune*.

Host Bill Cullen

As with many radio game shows, the transition to TV was inevitable. With a live house band providing the music, two contestants were challenged to ring a large bell and "Name that tune!" when they recognized the song being played. Winners received cash and the opponent with the most money proceeded to the "Golden Medley." This bonus round dared the winner to name seven songs in thirty seconds. If they did, they could take home $1600 – a sizable sum in the 1950s, where the median annual American income was slightly more than $2500.

Following a fifteen-year hiatus, *Name That Tune* returned to the tube, with Dennis James as host. The biggest change was the addition of the "Bid-A-Note" round, where players stood face-to-face and challenged each other to name a song with the fewest possible notes played on piano. By 1976, the syndicated series upped the ante to a potential jackpot of $100,000. Host Tom Kennedy ran the show, with a young and then-unknown Kathie Lee Johnson singing in the "Sing A Tune" segment (where lyrics were replaced with "la-las.") The blonde singer later became Kathie Lee Gifford when co-hosting *Live with Regis and Kathie Lee* for fifteen years.

Host Tom Kennedy

One more break in the schedule, this time for three years, saw a return to syndication with Jim Lange as host in 1984. The show lasted for only one season, although cable network VH1 delivered an updated version for the 21st Century. *Name That Video* used music videos to quiz contestants in 2001.

The Newlywed Game (First series)

July 11, 1966 – December 20, 1974 (8 seasons)

Network: ABC

Host(s): Bob Eubanks

Creator(s): Nick Nicholson, E. Roger Muir

Producer(s): Bill Carruthers, Walt Case, Mike Metzger

Director(s): Bill Carruthers, John Dorsey

The Newlywed Game (Second series)

January 7, 1967 – August 30, 1971 (5 seasons)

Network: ABC primetime

Host(s): Bob Eubanks

Creator(s): Nick Nicholson, E. Roger Muir

Producer(s): Bill Carruthers, Walt Case, Mike Metzger

Director(s): Bill Carruthers, John Dorsey

The Newlywed Game (Third series)

September 5, 1977 – September 1980 (4 seasons)

Network: Syndicated

Host(s): Bob Eubanks

Creator(s): Nick Nicholson, E. Roger Muir

Producer(s): Bill Carruthers, Walt Case, Mike Metzger

Director(s): Bill Carruthers, John Dorsey

The Newlywed Game (Fourth series)

February 13, 1984 – February 17, 1984 (1 week)

Network: ABC

Host(s): Jim Lange

Creator(s): Nick Nicholson, E. Roger Muir

Producer(s): Walt Case

Director(s): John Dorsey

The Newlywed Game (Fifth series)

September 16, 1985 – September 8, 1989 (4 seasons)

Network: Syndicated

Host(s): Bob Eubanks, Paul Rodriguez

Creator(s): Nick Nicholson, E. Roger Muir

Producer(s): Walt Case, Scott Sternberg, Bruce Starlin

Director(s): John Dorsey, Jeff Goldstein

The Newlywed Game (Sixth series)

September 9, 1996 – September 1999 (3 seasons)

Network:	Syndicated
Host(s):	Gary Kroeger (1996) Bob Eubanks (1997 – 1999)
Creator(s):	Nick Nicholson, E. Roger Muir
Producer(s):	Walt Case, Linda Lea
Director(s):	Paul Casey, Rob Fiedler

Host Bob Eubanks

Shortly after the success of the *Dating Game*, producer Chuck Barris hit upon another great idea. Get some newlywed couples together and ask them questions – find out what they really know about their new spouses. In fact, Barris was once quoted as saying, "Four couples, eight questions, and a washer/dryer – you had the perfect show." That perfect show was *The Newlywed Game*.

The couples were split up, with one gender sent to an isolated area, while the other answered questions – usually concerning previous relationships, the new in-laws, or sex (prohibited from saying "sex" or "making love," host Bob Eubanks immortalized the phrase, "making whoopee.") Once the answers were written down on cards, the sequestered spouses returned to see if their answers matched the ones given previously by the other spouse. Round one earned couples five points for every correct answer. Round two – where places were reversed – earned ten points for each match. The couple with the highest point total won the game and "a prize chosen just for you."

Barris knew that love was blind. And while it might not have been deaf, he quickly discovered from *The Newlywed* Game it was often DUMB. For example…

- EUBANKS: Husband number two, what is your favorite amphibian?

  ANSWER: My wife.

- EUBANKS: Husband number three, what's your favorite part of the *Newlywed Game* set?

  ANSWER: Wife number two.

- EUBANKS: Gentlemen, what Spanish word or phrase best describes your wife's bust?

  ANSWER: Nada. (Meaning "nothing.")

- EUBANKS: Ladies, what will your husband say is his favorite kind of rodent?

  ANSWER: What's a rodent? (PAUSE) His saxophone.

- EUBANKS: Ladies, what will your husband say is the one thing he absolutely forbids you to put on his wiener?

  ANSWER: Ben Gay.

- EUBANKS: Ladies, complete this sentence - "Most of the electricity in our home flows from the BLANK to the WHAT?

  ANSWER: From the plug to the vibrator.

- EUBANKS: In what country will your husband say the last foreign car he rode in was manufactured?

  ANSWER: Texas.

Couples on the *Newlywed Game* set

The Newlywed Game rolled along through the 60s, the 70s, and the 80s, all with host Bob Eubanks at the helm (with the exception of Jim Lange covering one week in 1984.) When producers played around with the show's format and replaced Eubanks with Paul Rodriguez in 1988, *The Newlywed Game* toppled like a fallen wedding cake. It was revived in 1996, but stayed – for better or for worse – for three seasons in the late 1990s, as Bob Eubanks returned to the podium.

The Price Is Right (First series)

November 26, 1956 – September 6, 1963 (7 seasons)

Network:	NBC
Host(s):	Bill Cullen
Creator(s):	Mark Goodson, Bill Todman, Bob Stewart
Producer(s):	Bob Stewart, Willie Stein, Beth Hollinger, Michael Graham
Director(s):	Max Miller, Don Bohl, Lou Tedesco, Paul Alter, Michael Graham

The Price Is Right (Second series)

September 23, 1957 – September 6, 1963 (6 seasons)

Network:	NBC primetime
Host(s):	Bill Cullen
Creator(s):	Mark Goodson, Bill Todman, Bob Stewart
Producer(s):	Bob Stewart, Willie Stein, Beth Hollinger, Michael Graham
Director(s):	Max Miller, Don Bohl, Lou Tedesco, Paul Alter, Michael Graham

The Price Is Right (Third series)

September 9, 1963 – September 3, 1965 (2 seasons)

Network:	ABC
Host(s):	Bill Cullen

Creator(s): Mark Goodson, Bill Todman, Bob Stewart

Producer(s): Bob Stewart, Willie Stein, Beth Hollinger, Michael Graham

Director(s): Max Miller, Don Bohl, Lou Tedesco, Paul Alter, Michael Graham

The Price Is Right (Fourth series)

September 9, 1963 – September 11, 1964 (1 season)

Network: ABC primetime

Host(s): Bill Cullen

Creator(s): Mark Goodson, Bill Todman, Bob Stewart

Producer(s): Bob Stewart, Willie Stein, Beth Hollinger, Michael Graham

Director(s): Max Miller, Don Bohl, Lou Tedesco, Paul Alter, Michael Graham

The Price Is Right (Fifth series)

September 4, 1972 –

Network: CBS

Host(s): Bob Barker (1972 – 2007) Drew Carey (2007)

Creator(s): Mark Goodson, Bill Todman, Bob Stewart

Producer(s): Jay Wolpert, Barbara Hunter, Phillip Wayne, Roger Dobkowitz

Director(s): Mark Breslow, Paul Alter

The Price Is Right (Sixth series)

September 11, 1972 – September 1979 (7 seasons)

Network: Syndicated

Host(s): Bob Barker

Creator(s): Mark Goodson, Bill Todman, Bob Stewart

Producer(s): Jay Wolpert, Barbara Hunter, Phillip Wayne, Roger Dobkowitz

Director(s): Mark Breslow, Paul Alter

The Price Is Right (Seventh series)

September 9, 1985 – September 5, 1986 (1 season)

Network: Syndicated

Host(s): Bob Barker

Creator(s): Mark Goodson, Bill Todman, Bob Stewart

Producer(s): Jay Wolpert, Barbara Hunter, Phillip Wayne, Roger Dobkowitz

Director(s): Mark Breslow, Paul Alter

The Price Is Right (Eighth series)

August 14, 1986 – September 18, 1986 (4 weeks)

Network: Syndicated

Host(s): Bob Barker

Creator(s): Mark Goodson, Bill Todman, Bob Stewart

Producer(s): Jay Wolpert, Barbara Hunter, Phillip Wayne, Roger Dobkowitz

Director(s): Mark Breslow, Paul Alter

The Price Is Right (Ninth series)

September 12, 1994 – January 27, 1995 (5 months)

Network: Syndicated

Host(s): Bob Barker

Creator(s): Mark Goodson, Bill Todman, Bob Stewart

Producer(s): Jay Wolpert, Barbara Hunter, Phillip Wayne, Roger Dobkowitz

Director(s): Mark Breslow, Paul Alter

The Price Is Right Million Dollar Spectacular (Tenth series)

February 22, 2008 – May 27, 2008 (3 months)

Network: CBS

Host(s): Drew Carey

Creator(s): Mark Goodson, Bill Todman, Bob Stewart

Producer(s): Jay Wolpert, Barbara Hunter, Phillip Wayne, Roger Dobkowitz

Director(s): Mark Breslow, Paul Alter

Many people believe that cats have nine lives. In the world of TV game shows, *The Price Is Right* has those felines beat by one. Except for a six-year break in the late 1960s, the show – in ten series – has had an amazing television presence for well over fifty years.

Host Bill Cullen & contestants

Four players looked at a prize, then bid on it – with the hopes of getting closest without going over the manufacturer's suggested retail price. The closest bidder won the prize. With ever-enthusiastic host Bill Cullen at the mike, *The Price Is Right* reigned in daytime and primetime spots for NBC and ABC for nearly ten years. At that time, the show offered home viewers a chance to get in on the action with a weekly Home Showcase. For example, with the theme of "wheels," one episode in 1958 offered the following seven items with wheels: a new Chrysler sedan, a bicycle, a tea cart, a golf hand cart, a half-sized French taxi, a riding lawn mower, and a new Chrysler 300-D convertible. Viewers attempting to correctly guess the total prices of those items (without going over,) sent in a postcard with their guess. The one closest to the penny won the entire package of prizes.

When *The Price Is Right* moved from NBC to ABC in 1963 (a common occurrence in those days,) a celebrity guest was added to the bidding panel – playing for an audience member or home viewer. The ABC version of *The Price Is Right* lasted until 1964 in primetime and 1965 in daytime.

When *The Price Is Right* returned in 1972 on CBS, it had a new format and a new host. Four audience members were famously invited to "Come on down!" and face newcomer host Bob Barker. The price bidding game now became a chance for the winner to join Barker on-stage for one of many different pricing games. The show also relied heavily on several

Bob Barker (L/R) Holly Hallstrom, Janice Pennington, & Dian Parkinson

lovely ladies to model and display the items offered for bidding. They became known as "Barker's Beauties;" Playboy model Janice Pennington and actress Anitra Ford were the first of many to grace the show.

Players had their favorite games. Some of the more popular ones included:

- *Hole In One* – Barker, an avid golfer who was featured as such in Adam Sandler's 1996 comedy *Happy Gilmore*, took pride in demonstrating how easy it was for a contestant to sink a putt – the distance was based on how well they priced grocery items.

- *Plinko* – Based on the Japanese toy called "pachinko," this game allowed players to earn Plinko chips by correctly guessing prices. Mounting a platform above an enormous peg-studded board, they dropped their chips – one at a time – with the hopes of landing in a money slot at the bottom of the board. This game could earn a player thousands of dollars.

- *Cliff Hangers* – A motorized yodeler climbed an inclined ramp, marked in dollar increments. A contestant guesses the prices of items and, for every dollar off from the actual price he or she is, the figure moved up the ramp toward a perilous fall. Hopefully, the contestant never got that far.

- *Dice Game* – The player was given the first number in the price of a brand new car. With four open chances on a price board (representing the remaining four numbers in the car price,) the player took one oversized dice and rolled it on a pint-sized craps table. Whatever number came up, the player was allowed to guess whether the next number in the car's price was higher or lower than that dice number. Once all four die were thrown, the actual price was revealed – with the player, hopefully, winning the car.

- *Punch-A-Bunch* – Shown four items, the player must decide whether the posted price is higher or lower than the actual price. For every correct answer, the player earned the chance to punch one of fifty paper-covered holes. Each hole contained a slip with a dollar amount – some as high as $10,000 or $25,000 (depending on the season of play.) With each amount revealed, the player could quit or trade it for the next – hoping for a higher amount.

Bob Barker & the Big Wheel

Top winners were given the chance to spin the Big Wheel – a large, carnival-like spinning device with amounts under $1.00. Players had two chances to get closest to a dollar without going over. Two closest found themselves in the Showcase Showdown, where they were shown two packages – usually with a vacation, furniture, boats, and/or cars. Each contestant bid a total value on a showcase and the closest (yes, yes – without going over) won the package.

Barker held court on *The Price Is Right* for thirty-five years. Nearly 84 years of age, he retired from the show in 2007 and the search began for his replacement. While Barker and his predecessor Cullen had been professional announcers and game show

Drew Carey (L/R) Brandi Sherwood, Gwendolyn Osborne, & Rachel Reynolds

hosts, the new host came from the world of standup and television comedy. Drew Carey was selected to lead the new season in the fall of 2007. The show continues to top the daytime television ratings.

No doubt, the price IS right.

To Tell The Truth (First series)

December 18, 1956 – September 25, 1966 (10 seasons)

Network: CBS primetime

Host(s): Bud Collyer

Creator(s): Mark Goodson, Bill Todman

Producer(s): Bob Stewart, Willie Stein, Bruno Zirato Jr.

Director(s): Franklin Heller, Paul Alter, Lloyd Gross

To Tell The Truth (Second series)

June 18, 1962 – September 6, 1968 (7 seasons)

Network: CBS

Host(s): Bud Collyer, Robert Q. Lewis

Creator(s): Mark Goodson, Bill Todman

Producer(s): Bob Stewart, Willie Stein, Bruno Zirato Jr.

Director(s): Franklin Heller, Paul Alter, Lloyd Gross

To Tell The Truth (Third series)

December 12, 1966 – May 22, 1967 (1season)

Network: CBS primetime

Host(s): Bud Collyer

Creator(s): Mark Goodson, Bill Todman

Producer(s): Bob Stewart, Willie Stein, Bruno Zirato Jr.

Director(s): Franklin Heller, Paul Alter, Lloyd Gross

To Tell The Truth (Fourth series)

September 8, 1969 – September 1978 (9 seasons)

Network: Syndicated

Host(s): Garry Moore, Bill Cullen, Joe Garagiola

Creator(s): Mark Goodson, Bill Todman

Producer(s): Bruno Zirato Jr.

Director(s): Paul Alter, Lloyd Gross

To Tell The Truth (Fifth series)

September 8, 1980 – September 4, 1981 (1 season)

Network: Syndicated

Host(s): Robin Ward

Creator(s): Mark Goodson, Bill Todman

Producer(s): Mimi O'Brien

Director(s): Lloyd Gross

To Tell The Truth (Sixth series)

September 3, 1990 – May 3, 1991 (1 season)

Network: NBC

Host(s): Gordon Elliott, Lynn Swann, Alex Trebek

Creator(s): Mark Goodson, Bill Todman

Producer(s): Mimi O'Brien

Director(s): Paul Alter

To Tell The Truth (Seventh series)

September 18, 2000 – March 1, 2002 (2 seasons)

Network: Syndicated

Host(s): John O'Hurley

Creator(s): Mark Goodson, Bill Todman

Producer(s): John Berkson, Rob Lloyd, Lisa Aline Schultz, Scott Smoley, Robert Taylor

Director(s): Kent Weed

One more from the "Kings of the Panel Show," Mark Goodson and Bill Todman, *To Tell The Truth* relied on celebrities' intuition, along with their ability to ask probing questions. Three strangers presented themselves as having a particular skill or fame – only one was actually who they claimed to be. The other two were impostors. The show gave birth to two of the more prominent catch-phrases of the day – "Will the REAL – (fill in the blank) please, stand up!" and "My name is…(again, fill in the blank.)"

Bud Collyer, radio's voice of *Superman*, hosted the original show in 1956, with a large variety of celebrities serving as guests on the panel. The spread included comedian Dick Van Dyke, spokesman extraordinaire John Cameron Swayze, actor Barry Nelson, singer Kitty Carlisle, Orson Bean and Peggy Cass (what DID they do, other than be game show panelists?), actor Don Ameche, comic and pie-thrower Soupy Sales, comic actor Tom Poston, comedian and film director Woody Allen, and many, many more.

Bud Collyer (L/R) Tom Poston, Kitty Carlisle, & Orson Bean

The stories told by the challengers – real and impostors – were just as diverse. For example, three lovely bathing-suit clad ladies all claimed to be Betsy Clark, a college student who rode Willie, a giant whale at a Philadelphia marine exhibit (three out of four panelists picked the wrong gal.) Three tall and brawny men said they were David Prowse, the man under the Darth Vader outfit in *Star Wars* (once again, three out of four chose the wrong guy.) Three George Burrows, all supposedly a campus cop at Harvard University – *and* the father of panelist Orson Bean – forced Bean to disqualify himself from participating (Two out of the three remaining panelists flagged the real pop.) Motown mogul Berry Gordy Jr. appeared, with two wannabes – while the Supremes sang "Baby Love." After a thorough grilling, the REAL Berry Gordy stood up, to the chagrin of all four incorrect panelists. The impostors were a doctor from Harlem Hospital and a hair stylist in New York City. Three men, two dressed sharply in suit and tie and one wearing a rumpled sport coat, open-collared shirt, and a mane of frizzled hair, all claimed to be the successful publisher of MAD magazine, William M. Gaines. Panelists went for the sharpest-dressed man and – you guessed it – Gaines turned out to be the Skid Row reject.

To Tell The Truth dominated CBS – both daytime and primetime – during the late 50s and through the 1960s. When it picked back up in syndication in 1968, Garry Moore hosted the show and, later, Bill Cullen and Joe Garagiola carried it to 1978. Syndication and NBC had their shots at the show in the 1980s and 1990s but – to tell the truth – it just wasn't the same any more.

Joe Garagiola (L/R) Peggy Cass, Bill Cullen, & Kitty Carlisle

?UESTIONS & ANSWERS

$64,000 Question

June 7, 1955 – June 24, 1958 (3 seasons)

Network: CBS primetime

Host(s): Hal March

Creator(s): Louis Cowan

Producer(s): Joe Cates, Mert Koplin

Director(s): Joe Cates, Curt Steen, Seymour Robbie

$64,000 Challenge (Spin-off)

April 8, 1956 – September 7, 1958 (2 seasons)

Network: CBS primetime

Host(s): Sonny Fox, Ralph Story

Creator(s): Louis Cowan

Producer(s): Joe Cates, Ed Jurist

Director(s): Joe Cates, Seymour Robbie

Once again, radio provided the origin for one of the most popular game shows of all time, as *Take It or Leave It* ran for seven years on the CBS radio network in the 1940s. The show then switched to NBC radio, where the name was changed to the more memorable *The $64 Question* in 1950.

Making the move to TV made sense, but $64 was hardly a sum that would excite potential viewers. Considering that the average American income in the 1950s was a little over $2,500, creator Louis Cowen figured $64,000 might raise some eyebrows. And it did.

Host Hal March

At one point in the success of *$64,000 Question*, an estimated 55 million Americans tuned in to watch. It was hosted by actor Hal March and offered a chance for topic experts to win a huge amount of money. Once the contestant chose their category (such as "Presidents," "Baseball," or "U.S. History,") they were asked questions of progressive difficulty. The first correct answer won the player $1, with each following correct answer doubling the winnings. At the level of $4,000, the contestant would return the following week for another question. Players could quit at any time with their winnings or press on toward the big question at $64,000. At $8,000, players were placed in an isolation booth and eligible for a brand new Cadillac if they missed any question along the way.

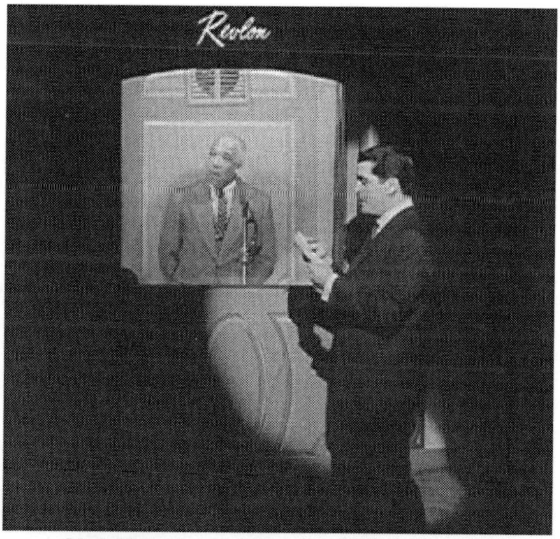

Hal March and the isolation booth

The show was big and players won big. Categories like cooking, boxing, opera, and Shakespeare earned players $64,000. The show's sponsor, Revlon, won big as well, seeing its sales triple in the second season of *$64,000 Question*. Producers received more than 20,000 letters a week from folks who wanted to appear on the show. It even produced a spin-off show: *The $64,000 Challenge* pitting contestants (including celebrities and former *Question* winners) against each other.

Unfortunately, it appears that producers and sponsor became too greedy, supplying answers to contestants prior to broadcast. As the quiz show scandals exploded in 1958, so did the success for *$64,000 Question* and the *$64,000 Challenge.*

Beat the Geeks

November 7, 2001 – October 7, 2002 (2 seasons)

Network: Comedy Central

Host(s): J. Keith van Straaten, Blaine Capatch

Creator(s): Mark Cronin, James Rowley

Producer(s): Richard King, Beth Greenbaum

Director(s): R. Brian DiPirro

One of the "hip" game shows to emerge in the 21st Century, *Beat the Geeks* gained a cult fan following in its two seasons on the Comedy Central cable channel. The show offered contestants the chance to, as the title simply suggested, beat geeky experts in categories such as movies, TV, and music, as well as specialties such as horror, *South Park*, James Bond, *the Simpsons*, and *Playboy* magazine, among others.

Hostess Tiffany Bolton, Geeks Mark Edward Heuck, Andy Zax, Paul Goebel

The opening round used pop-culture questions and answers to reduce the contestant count from three to two. These two players moved on to the second round, where they challenged the Geeks to protect their medals in head-to-head questioning. The player with the highest point total graduated to the final round, known as the "Geek-off." Choosing one Geek, the challenger answered one, two, or three point questions in an effort to total seven points. The Geek was pressed to answer questions of similar point values, with the first reaching the seven points declared the winner.

Beat the Geeks was hosted during its first season by J. Keith van Straaten, but was replaced by Blaine Capatch for the second season. Producers felt van Straaten just wasn't "geeky" enough for a show that had "Geek" in its title.

Host Blaine Capatch

Blockbusters (First series)

October 27, 1980 – April 23, 1982 (2 seasons)

Network: NBC

Host(s): Bill Cullen

Creator(s): Steve Ryan, Mark Goodson

Producer(s): Robert Sherman

Director(s): Ira Skutch

Blockbusters (Second series)

January 5, 1987 – May 1, 1987 (1 season)

Network: NBC

Host(s): Bill Rafferty

Creator(s): Steve Ryan, Mark Goodson

Producer(s): Diane Janaver

Director(s): Marc Breslow

With Bill Cullen hosting, viewers were always assured of a top-notch game show and *Blockbusters* was no exception. It was clearly one of the more unique and creative shows to kick off the 1980s.

A single contestant squared off against a pair of family-related opponents, with Cullen wondering if "two heads were better than one." A large grid of hexagons – five across by four down – had single letters in each figure.

Contestants would try to navigate the grid – the lone contestant seeking as few as four down, the team of two seeking as few as five across – by answering questions whose answers started with the chosen letter. For example – "What B attaches itself to the bottom of a ship?" A correct answer of "barnacle" gained the hexagon for the player.

Host Bill Cullen

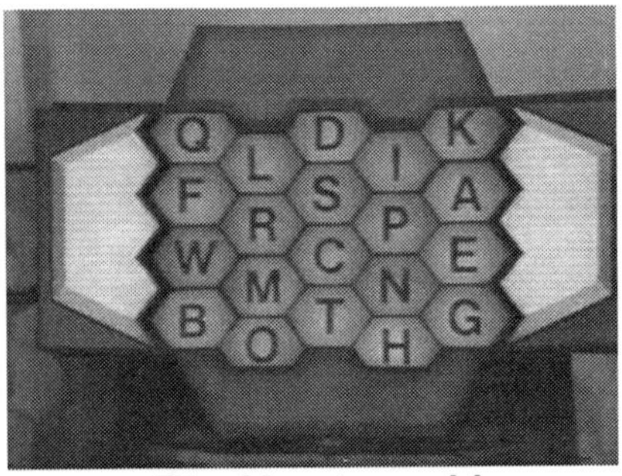

***Blockbusters* grid**

Winners of that round advanced to the "Gold Rush," where a single player attempted to cross the hexagonal grid by solving one or multi-lettered hexagons in sixty seconds. For example, "MT" was the current English Prime Minister (in 1980, it was "Margaret Thatcher.") Winners here would earn $2,500. When players won two games, they advanced to "Super Gold Rush," where the prize was $5,000. (The "Gold Rush" was inexplicably renamed the "Gold Run" during the first season.)

When *Blockbusters* returned to NBC after a five-year hiatus, Bill Rafferty was the host and the "one versus two" concept was abandoned for solo contestants.

Break the Bank (First series)

October 22, 1948 – September 23, 1949 (1 season)

Network: ABC primetime

Host(s): Bert Parks

Creator(s): Ed Wolf, Herb Wolf

Producer(s): Ed Wolf, Herb Wolf, Jack Rubin

Director(s): Marshall Dirkin, Craig Allen, Lloyd Gross

Break the Bank (Second series)

October 5, 1949 – January 9, 1952 (3 seasons)

Network: NBC primetime

Host(s): Bert Parks

Creator(s): Ed Wolf, Herb Wolf

Producer(s): Ed Wolf, Herb Wolf, Jack Rubin

Director(s): Marshall Dirkin, Craig Allen, Lloyd Gross

Break the Bank (Third series)

January 13, 1952 – February 1, 1953 (1 season)

Network: CBS primetime

Host(s): Bert Parks

Creator(s): Ed Wolf, Herb Wolf

Producer(s): Ed Wolf, Herb Wolf, Jack Rubin

Director(s): Marshall Dirkin, Craig Allen, Lloyd Gross

Break the Bank (Fourth series)

March 30, 1953 – September 18, 1953 (1 season)

Network: NBC

Host(s): Bud Collyer

Creator(s): Ed Wolf, Herb Wolf

Producer(s): Herb Wolf, Jack Rubin

Director(s): Craig Allen

Break the Bank (Fifth series)

June 23, 1953 – September 1, 1953 (1 season)

Network: NBC primetime

Host(s): Bert Parks

Creator(s): Ed Wolf, Herb Wolf

Producer(s): Herb Wolf, Jack Rubin

Director(s): Lloyd Gross, Matt Harlib

Break the Bank (Sixth series)

January 31, 1954 – June 20, 1956 (3 seasons)

Network: ABC primetime

Host(s): Bert Parks

Creator(s): Ed Wolf, Herb Wolf

Producer(s): Herb Wolf, Jack Rubin

Director(s): Lloyd Gross, Matt Harlib

Break the $250,000 Bank (Seventh series)

October 9, 1956 – January 15, 1957 (1 season)

Network: NBC primetime

Host(s): Bert Parks

Creator(s): Ed Wolf, Herb Wolf

Producer(s): Jack Rubin

Director(s): Lloyd Gross

Not to be confused with the game shows from the 1970s and 1980s with the same name (the only thing they had in common,) *Break the Bank* evolved from a 1945 radio show. The ever-congenial Bert Parks pulled contestants from the studio audience to answer questions worth $25 to $500. If answered correctly (allowing one miss,) the player had a shot at "breaking the bank" with another question. If they won, it meant at least $1,000 – the accumulated bank once reached more than $8,800.

During its initial nine-year run, *Break the Bank* bounced back and forth between ABC, NBC, and CBS like an unwanted pet. While it was never a top-rated show, *Break the Bank* had a steady audience and when it returned in the fall of 1956 amid the big money game shows, it became *Break the $250,000 Bank.* But the 3-1/2 month run wasn't enough to get anywhere close to the big money. The best any player reached was $60,000.

Host Bert Parks with contestants

College Bowl (First series)

January 4, 1959 – June 16, 1963 (5 seasons)

Network: CBS

Host(s): Allen Ludden, Robert Earle

Creator(s): Don Reid

Producer(s): John Cleary

Director(s): Lamar Caselli, Robert Hultgren

College Bowl (Second series)

September 22, 1963 – June 14, 1970 (7 seasons)

Network: NBC

Host(s): Robert Earle

Creator(s): Don Reid

Producer(s): John Cleary

Director(s): Lamar Caselli, Robert Hultgren

College Bowl (Third series)

September 13, 1987 – December 20, 1987 (1 season)

Network: Disney Channel

Host(s): Dick Cavett

Creator(s): Don Reid

Producer(s): Mary Oberembt

Director(s): Dennis Rosenblatt

Host Allen Ludden with 1961 winning team

Host Allen Ludden first brought *College Bowl* to the airwaves via radio in 1953, where two teams of college students faced off answering questions asked by Ludden. Amazingly (for the time,) Ludden was in a New York studio, while Northwestern University students were in Evanston, Illinois and Columbia University students were on the Manhattan campus in New York City. All three were hooked up by radio lines. Winning teams picked up $500 grants for their respective schools.

The show hit the TV airwaves in 1959, sponsored by General Electric. Thus, the program became known as the *G.E. College Bowl*. Winnings were increased to $1,500 (later $3,000) in scholarships.

In one of the great "David meets Goliath" meetings of all time, tiny Agnes Scott College – located near Atlanta, Georgia – took on the powerhouse of Princeton University in the spring of 1966. The all-woman Agnes Scott team trailed Princeton with only two minutes left, but hit two final correct answers to scratch out the amazing victory.

College Bowl returned for a special show in 1978 and again in 1984. It reappeared on a regular basis in 1987, hosted by Dick Cavett on the Disney Channel cable outlet, broadcasting from DisneyWorld in Orlando, Florida.

Live production of the *G.E. College Bowl*

Do You Trust Your Wife?

January 3, 1956 – March 26, 1957 (2 seasons)

Network:	CBS primetime
Host(s):	Edgar Bergen (with Charlie McCarthy, Mortimer Snerd, and Effie Klinker)
Creator(s):	Fred Henry
Producer(s):	Don Fedderson
Director(s):	Jim Morgan, Fred Henry

Who Do You Trust?

September 30, 1957 – December 27, 1963 (6 seasons)

Network:	ABC
Host(s):	Johnny Carson, Woody Woodbury
Creator(s):	Fred Henry
Producer(s):	Jim Morgan, Art Stark, Jim Landis
Director(s):	Al Burton, David Lowe

This is a title that clearly reflects the second-place position unfairly given to American women in the 1950s. No matter, *Do You Trust Your Wife?* was a show that drew its inspiration from Groucho Marx and *You Bet Your Life*. Like that show, *Do You Trust Your Wife?* (and its successor, *Who Do You Trust*?) relied on a clever and witty host that could make interesting conversation with the guests.

Edgar Bergen was a ventriloquist, well-known as a radio and film star, who funneled his rapier wit through dummies Charlie McCarthy, Mortimer Snerd, and Effie Klinker. On *Do You Trust Your Wife?* the team met husband and wife contestants, usually couples with unique and unusual interests. For example, one couple ran a chicken farm in southern California (to which dim-witted Mortimer Snerd replied, "Well, shake hands – I'm foul-minded, too.") Another couple, originally from Sweden, came on – and were immediately welcomed in fluent Swedish by Bergen (as well as the wooden-headed Charlie McCarthy, who anxiously asked his boss, "What did you just make me say?") Coincidentally, Bergen had been born to a Swedish family.

Charlie McCarthy, Edgar Bergen, & Mortimer Snerd

The game that followed seemed like an afterthought. Bergen would ask four questions, with the husband answering them or – how generous – trusting his wife to do so. Each correct response earned \$100, \$200, and \$300. The final question gave the option of risking some or all of the amassed \$600. The big winners of the week had the chance to win \$100 a week for a year by answering a final "Trust Fund Question."

The show moved from CBS primetime to ABC daytime in the fall of 1957. Bergen was replaced by a young and clever comic named Johnny Carson. He was a natural for the now-politically correct title of *Who Do You Trust?* (although several episodes were still titled *Do You Trust Your Wife?*) When Carson left for the *Tonight Show* (along with announcer Ed McMahon) in 1962, stand-up comic Woody Woodbury hosted for the remaining two seasons.

Greed

November 4, 1999 – July 14, 2000 (1 season)

Network: FOX

Host(s): Chuck Woolery

Creator(s): Bob Boden, Dick Clark

Producer(s): Larry Klein

Director(s): Chris Donovan, Bob Levy

Host Chuck Woolery

Hot on the heels of the successful *Who Wants to Be A Millionaire?*, the Fox Network delivered *Greed* in fall of 1999. The affable Chuck Woolery hosted the show, complete with ominous sounds and dramatic lighting.

Five contestants worked as a team to climb eight levels of multiple-choice questions, with values starting at $25,000 and increasing to $2 million. The "Captain" of the team, determined by an initial question, had the option of accepting each member's answer to a question or overriding it and providing an alternate response. However, a head-to-head challenge called the "Terminator" pared down the team by pitting two players against each other, with the challenger taking $10,000 – win or lose.

The success of the game was based on the team's ability to agree on correct answers, as well as come up with them. More than once, television cameras captured the glaring anger of a player who watched as the captain

***Greed* contestants**

agreed with a wrong answer – immediately losing the game for the entire team.

If a team won the $1 million question, each player was given the option of taking their share and quitting or going on to the $2 million question. Only one player ever reached this level – alone – and missed.

Greed became *Super Greed* in its last two months, offering as much as $4 million. But *Greed's* appeal fell as quickly as it grew. Even though a second season was announced, it left the Fox airwaves in July of 2000.

Jeopardy! (First series)

March 30, 1964 – January 3, 1975 (12 seasons)

Network: NBC

Host(s): Art Fleming

Creator(s): Merv Griffin

Producer(s): Robert Rubin, Lynette Williams

Director(s): Bob Hultgren, Eleanor Tarshis, Jeff Goldstein

Jeopardy! (Second series)

September 9, 1974 – September 7, 1975 (1 season)

Network: Syndicated

Host(s): Art Fleming

Creator(s): Merv Griffin

Producer(s): Robert Rubin, Lynette Williams

Director(s): Bob Hultgren, Eleanor Tarshis, Jeff Goldstein

Jeopardy! (Third series)

October 2, 1978 – March 2, 1979 (1 season)

Network: NBC

Host(s): Art Fleming

Creator(s): Merv Griffin

Producer(s): George Vosburgh

Director(s): Jeff Goldstein

Jeopardy! (Fourth series)

September 17, 1984 - Present (25 seasons)

Network: Syndicated

Host(s): Alex Trebek

Creator(s): Merv Griffin

Producer(s): Alex Trebek, George Vosburgh, Brett Schneider, Deb Dittman

Director(s): Dick Schneider, Kevin McCarthy

Creator Merv Griffin credited his wife with the distinction of thinking up a game show where the contestants asked questions to given answers. It would become what many people believe is the most successful television game show in history.

This…is…*Jeopardy!*

Now in its fifth decade of production, *Jeopardy!* relies on fast reflexes and faster minds for its success. Three contestants play two rounds, choosing from a gridboard of thirty questions – five each in six different categories. The third round, called "Final Jeopardy!" allows the players to wager any or all of their winnings on a single question in a single category.

Hosted by Art Fleming in the 1960s and 70s, the show started with modest amounts for its five progressive questions - $10 to $50. In "Double Jeopardy," the figures (appropriately) doubled. By the time Alex Trebek entered his 18th season as host in 2001, the numbers had risen to $200 to $1000 for "Jeopardy" and $400 to $2000 for the second round. Such increases (along with the elimination of the five-day limit for returning champions) allowed Ken Jennings to earn an incredible $2,520,700 in 74 consecutive wins on *Jeopardy!* in 2004.

Host Art Fleming

Host Alex Trebek & contestants

A reasonable amount of mental firepower is required to play and win at *Jeopardy!* Categories have been as vast and varied as "Potent Potables" (answers about alcoholic beverages,) "Those Darn Etruscans" (a category about ancient Roman society,) "Potpourri" (a hodge-podge of answers,) "Poet-pourri" (assorted answers about poets,) "Four-Letter Words" (answers with, obviously, four letters,) among many thousands of other topics. Tougher answers may have included:

- Geography – "It's the only state lying south of the Tropic of Cancer." (What is "Hawaii?")

- The Civil War – "This abolitionist congressman from Pennsylvania insisted on being buried in an integrated cemetery." (Who was "Thaddeus Stevens?")

- Aviation – "Some claim that the Wright brothers made only a power glider and that this Brazilian really invented the airplane. (Who was "Albert Santos-Dumont?")

Of course, "tough" was only relative to a player's body of knowledge.

In nearly forty seasons of *Jeopardy!* there's bound to have been a few odd questions – even for champions. Ken Jennings nearly brought down the house during his famous string of wins by responding to this answer under the "Tool Time" category: "This term for a long-handled gardening tool can also mean an immoral pleasure seeker" with "What is a hoe?" (The correct question was "What is a rake?") Another answer offered, "By the 4th century AD, Rome had 28 public ones stacked with rolls of papyrus." The player queried, "What are public toilets?" (The correct question was "What are public libraries?") Alex Trebek once offered, "If a Japanese "isha" (doctor) asks you to stick out your "shita", he means this." The player asked "What is your behind?" (He misunderstood the Japanese word "shita," which means "tongue.")

Champion Ken Jennings

Few TV game shows have the staying power and appeal that *Jeopardy!* has shown. In more than 8,000 episodes in its history, *Jeopardy!* has never been afraid to stay fresh, adding audio and video answers, as well as a diverse "Clues Crew" and tournaments featuring former champions, teens, college students, and celebrities. At the same time, the basis of the game has remained – give the player the answer and let them ask the question.

<u>Sale of the Century</u> (First series)

September 29, 1969 – July 13, 1973 (4 seasons)

Network: NBC

Host(s): Jack Kelly, Joe Garagiola

Creator(s): William Jones, Al Howard

Producer(s): Ron Greenberg, Willie Stein

Director(s): Paul Alter, Mike Garguilo

<u>Sale of the Century</u> (Second series)

September 10, 1973 – September, 1974 (1 season)

Network: Syndicated

Host(s): Joe Garagiola

Creator(s): William Jones, Al Howard

Producer(s): Ron Greenberg, Willie Stein

Director(s): Paul Alter, Mike Garguilo

<u>Sale of the Century</u> (Third series)

January 3, 1983 – March 24, 1989 (7 seasons)

Network: NBC

Host(s): Jim Perry

Creator(s): William Jones, Al Howard

Producer(s): George Vosburgh, Burt Wheeler

Director(s): Jerome Shaw, James Marcione

Three contestants answered simple questions, earning anywhere from $5 to $15 for each correct answer. As they built their banks of cash, players would be offered "Instant Bargains," where they could spend their money – at great discounts. For example, a Hawaiian vacation valued at more than $2,100 could be had for a mere $17 – all on *Sale of the Century*.

Play continued until the top money-earner got the chance to spend it all at the "Sale of the Century." Of course, the dilemma facing the champ was to spend at that moment or take the chance of winning another game and buying more at the big sale. Bargains could be had, for example - a $3,000 living room for $85, or a $12,000 diamond pendant for $445, or a $21,000 sailboat for $326, or even a $40,000 Mercedes-Benz for $390. Add a potential cash jackpot of $50,000 (or up to $100,000) and it's easy to see why *Sale of the Century* was a popular game – for players and viewers alike.

On the set of *Sale of the Century*

Originally hosted by Jack Kelly (formerly the television cowboy "Maverick",) *Sale of the Century* was taken over by ex-major league catcher Joe Garagiola in 1971. When the show returned in the 1980s, former Broadway singer Jim Perry brought his persuasive skills to encourage players to cut deals and make their bargains bigger.

Tic Tac Dough (First series)

July 30, 1956 – October 23, 1959 (3 seasons)

Network: NBC

Host(s): Jack Barry, Gene Rayburn, Bill Wendell

Creator(s): Jack Barry, Dan Enright

Producer(s): Howard Felsher

Director(s): Edward King, Hudson Fausett, Garry Simpson, Richard Auerbach

Tic Tac Dough (Second series)

September 12, 1957 – December 29, 1958 (2 seasons)

Network: NBC primetime

Host(s): Jay Jackson, Win Elliott

Creator(s): Jack Barry, Dan Enright

Producer(s): Howard Felsher

Director(s): Edward King, Hudson Fausett, Garry Simpson, Richard Auerbach

Tic Tac Dough (Third series)

July 3, 1978 – September 1, 1978 (2 months)

Network: CBS

Host(s): Wink Martindale

Creator(s): Jack Barry, Dan Enright

Producer(s): Ron Greenberg, Allen Koss, Chris Sohl

Director(s): Richard Kline, D.A. Diana

<u>Tic Tac Dough</u> (Fourth series)

September 18, 1978 – September, 1986 (8 seasons)

Network: Syndicated

Host(s): Wink Martindale, Jim Caldwell

Creator(s): Jack Barry, Dan Enright

Producer(s): Ron Greenberg, Allen Koss, Chris Sohl

Director(s): Richard Kline, D.A. Diana

<u>Tic Tac Dough</u> (Fifth series)

September 10, 1990 – March 8, 1991 (1 season)

Network: Syndicated

Host(s): Patrick Wayne

Creator(s): Jack Barry, Dan Enright

Producer(s): Chris Sohl

Director(s): Michael Dimich

With an obvious, yet clever play on words for a title, *Tic Tac Dough* was *Hollywood Squares* without the celebrities. Two players took turns answering questions to earn an "X" or an "O' in a tic-tac-toe grid, filled with a variety of question categories. The first with three in a row or a majority of squares won the game and cash.

***Tic Tac Dough* gameboard in 1980**

The NBC primetime version became part of the quiz show scandals, as producer Howard Felsher admitted to a congressional committee that three-quarters of the nighttime *Tic Tac Dough* shows had been rigged. Felsher was fired by NBC, although the daytime version was untouched by the scandal.

Thom McKee & Wink Martindale

When the show returned in 1978 after a near twenty-year absence, Wink Martindale hosted. A bonus round was added, as a single player picked squares from the grid one at a time – behind each square was a cash amount between $100 and $500, along with a "tic" and a "tac" (selecting both immediately won the round and earned the player $1,000.) But there was also a "dragon" hiding on the board – finding this square killed the round and the player lost any cash gained during the round.

If a player won five matches in a row, they won a new car. As the show had no limit of wins, many players won multiple matches. They accumulated several cars and cash, sometimes totaling more than $100,000 – an amazing amount for 1980s game shows. One player, Thom McKee, won eight cars and more than $200,000 in cash in 1980, defeating 43 players in a period of nine weeks.

Tic Tac Dough holds the distinction of being one of the first game shows to use computer-generated graphics. Starting in 1980, each of the nine squares was controlled by an Apple II computer, displaying colorful (if limited) images and text.

Much better than the old standby of pencil and paper.

<u>Twenty-One</u> (First series)

September 12, 1956 – October 16, 1958 (3 seasons)

Network: NBC primetime

Host(s): Jack Barry

Creator(s): Robert Noah

Producer(s): Howard Merrill, Al Freedman

Director(s): Charles Dubin, Al Freedman

<u>Twenty-One</u> (Second series)

January 9, 2000 – May 28, 2000 (1 season)

Network: NBC primetime

Host(s): Maury Povich

Creator(s): Robert Noah

Producer(s): David Floyd

Director(s): Bob McKinnon

This is the 1950s game show that launched a 1994 feature film. *Twenty-One*, the show that made Charles Van Doren a household name, became *Quiz Show*, a fascinating movie directed by Robert Redford. Ralph Fiennes, as Van Doren, and John Tuturro, as deposed champ Herb Stempel, turned in outstanding performances.

The game of *Twenty-One* placed two contestants in isolation booths, where they answered questions in varied categories valued from one to eleven points. The higher the point value, the more difficult the question. The first player to reach 21 points won the game. It was a game of high pressure, with big money payoffs for the winners. Unfortunately, the show didn't start out that way.

Played straight, the first broadcast of *Twenty-One* was, according to producer Dan Enright, "a dismal failure…just plain dull." Contestants were embarrassingly bad, lacking the knowledge to answer the questions correctly and the ability to create any suspense or excitement. The sponsor, Geritol, was not pleased, telling Enright they "never wanted to see a repeat of what happened." From then on, contestants were coached – with categories, questions, answers, and how to answer them.

Charles Van Doren, hostess, Jack Barry & Herb Stempel

Herb Stempel was one of those contestants. Gifted with an enormous body of knowledge, he was nevertheless told when to breathe heavily and when to mop his brow when answering questions. In six weeks, he had won nearly $70,000 on *Twenty-One*. The show's producers, figuring the nerdish Stempel had outlived his usefulness, chose Charles Van Doren – handsome college instructor and son of Pulitzer Prize-winning poet Mark Van Doren – to defeat him. Enright convinced Van Doren that "coaching" was a common practice and he became an immediate sensation. The likable Van Doren appeared on the cover of *Time* magazine and gained a regular spot on NBC's *Today Show*. For TV viewers, Van Doren had become the hero and Stempel the villain.

Tension was built with tie games, until Stempel was told to lose by Enright. He reluctantly did as he was told and, as Van Doren racked up $129,000 – along with book offers and marriage proposals – Stempel stewed in the fact that he had been used. He took his story to a newspaper, but they brushed it off as phony. But when the story about the rigging of *Dotto* broke, Stempel's story of fixing was taken as fact. Game shows, including *Twenty-One*, began falling out of the broadcast schedules. Once the congressional hearings were completed, Charles Van Doren pled guilty to lying under oath and received a suspended sentence. Herb Stempel went to college on his GI Bill and became a New York City school teacher.

New champion Vivian Nearing, Jack Barry & Charles Van Doren

And *Twenty-One* left the airwaves – for 42 years. In the wake of big-buck game shows like *Who Wants to Be A Millionaire* and *Greed*, NBC resurrected *Twenty-One* in 2000. News anchor Maury Povich kept the show above reproach for the five months it was on the air.

Who Wants to Be A Millionaire? (First series)

August 16, 1999 – July 14, 2002 (3 seasons)

Network:	ABC primetime
Host(s):	Regis Philbin
Creator(s):	David Briggs, Mike Whitehill, Steve Knight
Producer(s):	Michael Davies
Director(s):	Mark Gentile

Who Wants to Be A Millionaire? (Second series)

September 16, 2002 – Present

Network:	Syndicated
Host(s):	Meredith Vieira
Creator(s):	David Briggs, Mike Whitehill, Steve Knight
Producer(s):	Michael Davies, Leigh Hampton, Rich Sirop, Tiffany Trigg
Director(s):	Matthew Cohen

It was a phrase that became part of the American lexicon – "Is that your final answer?" It was a show that captured the interest of more than 30 million viewers every night – for as many as four times a week. It was a program that really gave players the chance to win serious – SERIOUS – money.

It was *Who Wants to Be A Millionaire?*

Originally a show in the UK that offered one million pounds in 1998, *Who Wants to Be A Millionaire?* quickly grabbed the attention of American viewers in 1999. The show's premise was simple – one player answered fifteen multiple-choice questions of increasing difficulty, picking up cash (in approximate multiples – for example, winning $500 lead to the $1,000 question; winning $125,000 lead to the $250,000 question and so on.) The last question was played for $1 million.

Getting to the show was not so simple. During its primetime run, prospective contestants called a special toll-free number during specific time periods, using their telephone touch pads to arrange four answers in three separate questions in correct order. Those who were successful were placed in a pool, where they would be randomly selected to receive a phone call at a later time. Those receiving that call were given a private number and time to dial in, where they would answer five more questions. If the player was successful at that level, they still had to be one of ten random selections to actually play the game on the air. Winners (and a companion) would be flown to New York City, chauffered to a posh hotel, where they were put up for three days, given stipend money for meals – and the chance to win $1 million on national television.

Host Regis Philbin

Talk show host and celebrity Regis Philbin was chosen to host the show, where his "everyman" personality and genuine lack of knowledge of some of the questions and answers resonated with many viewers. Philbin helped players through the ominous music and flashing lights, encouraging them to use "Lifelines" when needed. Contestants could "Ask the Audience" to assist in picking the answer, ask for the "50/50," which eliminated two of the answers, and "Phone A Friend," where assistance could be gained from calling pre-arranged help.

Make no mistake - *Who Wants to Be A Millionaire?* was a tough game show. But players across the years have sometimes made it tougher than it needed to be. One young fellow had the following for the first question, worth $100: "Homeowners buy surge protectors to protect their possessions from unexpected surges of what? A: Electric current B: Water flow C: Air pressure or D: Buyer's remorse." The lad quickly answered "B" – and look on his face was priceless when told that A was the answer. A young woman tackled this $200 question: "What punctuation mark is commonly used to introduce a list of items? A: Colon B: Apostrophe C: Period or D: Exclamation point." The correct answer of A eluded her for some reason, as she replied, "C – period."

John Carpenter

On the other side, *Millionaire* offered rare moments in winning huge amounts of money. The very first million-dollar winner, John Carpenter, created an unforgettable moment when asked the million-dollar question, "Which of these U.S. Presidents appeared on the television series 'Laugh-In'? A: Lyndon Johnson B: Richard Nixon C: Jimmy Carter or D: Gerald Ford?" Carpenter asked to use his lifeline to call his dad. Once hooked up, he shocked America by saying, "Hi, dad – I don't really need your help. I just wanted to let you know I'm going to win a million dollars." The audience erupted in laughter and applause, while Philbin grinned. When Carpenter coolly answered, "Richard Nixon – That's my final answer," America realized that $1 million could be as close as a trip to NYC.

While the syndicated daytime version continues to this day (with Meredith Vieria hosting, bringing an intellectual manner and good looks with her,) the ABC primetime version burned out after three seasons. The network saturated the public with the show, running it as many as three and four times a week. *Millionaire* left as quickly as it arrived – Easy come, easy go.

Win Ben Stein's Money

July 28, 1997 – December 31, 2002 (6 seasons)

Network: Comedy Central

Host(s): Ben Stein

Creator(s): Al Burton

Producer(s): Byron Glore, Andrew J. Golder

Director(s): Dennis Rosenblatt

Hosts and hostesses on game shows have usually been congenial and good-looking, but not necessarily high in the IQ department (with some exceptions, like Bill Cullen.) Cable network Comedy Central changed that dynamic, making brilliant and scholarly Ben Stein the host of *Win Ben Stein's Money* in 1997. To make matters worse – contestants had to BEAT Stein to earn up to $5,000.

Ben Stein

A top graduate from Yale Law School, Stein has been an attorney, a college professor, and a speechwriter for U.S. President Richard Nixon. He also authored books on economics before hitting the silver screen in 1986 as a dull and monotone high school teacher in *Ferris Bueller's Day Off.* There was no question about Stein's intellectual and academic qualifications.

Heavy on the humor (courtesy of co-hosts Jimmy Kimmel, Nancy Pimental, and Sal Iacono,) the show kept its tongue firmly in its cheek while asking general knowledge questions of three contestants. Some of the more original categories were:

- Don't Cry for Me, Ike and Tina
- Borneo, Borneo, Wherefore Art Thou Borneo
- He Plays Blackjack in His Shirtsleeves and Craps in His Pants
- If You Da Pimp, Idaho
- Like a Rhinestone Cow Pie

Win Ben Stein's Money was also very touchy about being confused with other game shows. If a player answered in the form of a question (ala *Jeopardy!*) he or she was given a dunce cap that had to be worn for the rest of the round.

Ben Stein & Jimmy Kimmel

Two of the three contestants moved from the first to the second round, where they went against Stein, who feigned arrogance and contempt at having to post $5,000 of his money as a prize (it was actually money posted by the producers – if the contestants didn't win it, then it went to Stein.) The player who accrued the most money wound up head-to-head against Ben in the "Best of Ten Test of Knowledge." Each was placed in an isolation booth – Ben's was lavish, while the opponent's looked like it was kept by a slumlord. No matter, they each were asked ten questions – if the opponent gave more correct answers than Stein, the $5,000 was theirs.

The show enjoyed a six season run, during which it won seven Emmy Awards. It's also not well known that Ben Stein donated all of his prize winnings to charities.

THAT WAS A SHOW TOO?

That Was A Show Too?

For every hit game show on the air, there might have been five or ten that landed in the world of obscurity. Not every show could be *The Price Is Right, Jeopardy!*, or *To Tell the Truth*.

Some of these programs were attempts by a network to cash in on a current fad or popular show on another channel. Others were efforts by syndicators to produce inexpensive and quick programming for sale to local TV stations. Nevertheless, game shows like these also hold a place in broadcat history.

Anyone Can Win

July 14, 1953 – September 1, 1953 (3 months)

Network: CBS primetime

Host(s): Al Capp

Al Capp had gained his fame as the cartoonist of the "Lil' Abner" comic strip. In hosting this summer show, Capp asked four celebrities questions in various topics. Prior to starting, the studio audience was polled to pick the celebrity who would

Anyone Can Win **panel**

answer the most questions correctly. Those who picked the right celeb divvied up $2,000.

Bingo-At-Home

Host Monty Hall

February 18, 1958 - December 12, 1958 (1 season)

Network: WABD-TV, New York City

Host(s): Monty Hall

Following a budding career in Canadian radio and television, Monty Hall hosted a local NYC game show called *Bingo-At-Home*. It was an early experiment in interactive TV - with no studio audience, Hall would call out Bingo numbers and home viewers tried to match them with the last five digits of their telephone number.

Bride and Groom

Bride and Groom

January 25, 1951 – 1954 (4 seasons)

Network: CBS (1951 - 1953)
NBC (1954)

Host(s): John Nelson

Bride and Groom was an early peek into reality TV, as couples united in matrimony on the national airwaves. A Christian or Jewish ceremony followed an interview session, where the husband and bride-to-be discussed their dreams. After they said, "I do," the newlyweds received a honeymoon and gifts from the network.

Chance of A Lifetime

Chance of A Lifetime

September 6, 1950 – June 23, 1956 (7 seasons)

Network: ABC primetime (1950 - 1953, 1955 - 1956) DuMont primetime (1953 - 1955)

Host(s): John Reed King, Dennis James

The first two seasons of this show combined question-answering and stunt-performing. When it returned, new host Dennis James offered talent - such as singers, dancers, and musicians - the *Chance of A Lifetime* to win cash and a shot at stardom, more than fifty years before Fox's *American Idol.*

Face Is Familiar

June Lockhart & Bob Crane

May 7, 1966 - September 3, 1966 (1 season)

Network: CBS primetime

Host(s): Jack Whitaker

Pairing a celebrity such as Carol Burnett or Bob Crane and studio contestant, *The Face Is Familiar* showed bits and pieces of pictures on a screen, while the teams tried to identify the person in the photo. Sportscaster Jack Whitaker awarded cash to the winning team.

<u>Giant Step</u>

Host Bert Parks with young contestant

November 7, 1956 - May 29, 1957 (1 season)

Network: CBS primetime

Host(s): Bert Parks

Giant Step was a pint-sized version of the *$64,000 Question*. Students from grade school to high school age answered questions in their chosen category, with the goal of winning a full, four-year college scholarship. As tension built along the way, contestants won prizes.

Host Bob Warren

<u>What Are the Odds</u>

1958 (1 season)

Network: Syndicated

Host(s): Bob Warren

Not so much a game show as it was a newsreel-type show with facts and figures, *What*

Are the Odds presented pre-produced vignettes narrated by Bob Warren. The host presented estimates and probabilities, including reassuring thoughts such as, "The odds are 100,000 to one against your being in a train wreck."

What's Your Bid

February 14, 1953 - June 29, 1953 (1 season)

Network: ABC primetime/DuMont primetime

Host(s): Liberal Bill (Leonard Rosen)

Host "Liberal Bill"

It certainly wasn't eBay, but *What's Your Bid* offered live auctions to studio audiences, who used their own money to win prizes on the auction block. Winning bids went to charity, all under the watchful eye of auctioneer "Liberal Bill," who ended each auction with an irritating "shave-and-a-haircut" pounding of his gavel.

Who Said That?

December 9, 1948 - July 26, 1955 (7 seasons)

Network: NBC primetime (1948 - 1954) ABC primetime (1955)

***Who Said That?* panel**

Host(s): Robert Trout, Walter Kiernan, John Charles Daly

Combining current events and quiz show, *Who Said That?* challenged a panel of newspeople and celebrities to correctly identify quotes from recent headlines. Wrong answers resulted in money contributions that went to charity or home viewers.

Hosts With The Most

NAME: Bob Barker (Robert William Barker)

BIRTHDATE: December 12, 1923

BIRTHPLACE: Darrington, Washington

MAJOR GAME SHOWS: *Truth Or Consequences* (1956 – 1975), *The Price Is Right* (1972 – 2007)

If TV game shows were track events, then Bob Barker would be a marathon specialist. Originally a fighter pilot in WWII and a radio announcer, Barker's near-twenty year tenure with *Truth Or Consequences* and thirty-five year run with *The Price Is Right* were unprecedented in TV history.

With a commanding presence, Barker emceed the wacky stunts of *Truth Or Consequences*, concluding each show with a positive note – "This is Bob Barker saying good-bye, hoping all your consequences are happy ones!" His dominance on *The Price Is Right* empowered him to wage war on the front of animal rights, reminding viewers to "help control the pet population by having your pet spayed or neutered."

NAME: Jack Barry (Jack Barasch)

BIRTHDATE: March 20, 1918

DATE OF DEATH: May 2, 1984

BIRTHPLACE: Lindenhurst, Long Island, New York

MAJOR GAME SHOWS: *Tic Tac Dough* (1956 – 1958), *Twenty-One* (1956 – 1958), *Concentration* (1958), *Joker's Wild* (1972 – 1975, 1977 - 1984)

A graduate of the prestigious University of Pennsylvania's Wharton School of Finance and Commerce, Jack Barry used his smarts to become an innovator in TV game shows. It was those same smarts that got him into hot water, too.

Working with partner Dan Enright, Barry created some of the first big-money game shows like *Tic-Tac-Dough* and *Twenty-One*. But a fateful matchup of contestants Charles Van Doren and Herb Stempel lead to the quiz show scandals, cancelling the shows and sending Barry into seclusion. He later admitted he learned of the rigged shows AFTER they had been already set up. Blackballed in the industry, Barry scuffled around for a few years, then struck gold with *The Joker's Wild.* Barry later revived *Tic-Tac-Dough*, hosted by Wink Martindale.

Jack Barry suffered a massive heart attack while jogging in New York and died in 1984.

NAME: Dick Clark (Richard Wagstaff Clark)

BIRTHDATE: November 30, 1929

BIRTHPLACE: Mount Vernon, New York

MAJOR GAME SHOWS: *The $10,000 Pyramid* (1973 – 1976), *The $20,000 Pyramid* (1976 – 1980), *The $50,000 Pyramid* (1981), *The $25,000 Pyramid* (1982 – 1987) *The $100,000 Pyramid* (1985 – 1988)

Better known for his association with the music world and *American Bandstand* (as well as watching the ball drop in Times Square on New Year's Eve,) Dick Clark has left a lasting mark on TV game shows as host of the *Pyramid* series.

A graduate of Syracuse University, Clark became a radio disc jockey in Philadelphia and soon began hosting *American Bandstand*. It was a role he would hold for more than thirty years. He also began hosting *The $10,000 Pyramid* for CBS in 1973. His cool demeanor and always-youthful looks kept him popular with viewers. As the program changed networks and dollar values, Clark remained host for the next fifteen years.

NAME:	Bud Collyer (Clayton Johnson Heermance, Jr.)
BIRTHDATE:	June 8, 1908
DATE OF DEATH:	September 8, 1969
BIRTHPLACE:	New York, New York
MAJOR GAME SHOWS:	*Beat The Clock* (1950 – 1958), *To Tell The Truth* (1956 – 1968)

Clayton Heermance Jr. started out as a law clerk after graduating from Fordham University, but his strong voice was a natural for radio. Taking his mother's maiden name and his own nickname, Bud Collyer became known in 1940 as the voice of the "Man of Steel," Superman, on radio and in movie theater cartoons.

After hosting several radio quiz shows, Collyer took on the hosting chores for TV's primetime *Beat The Clock* in 1950. As difficult as many of the zany stunts were, Collyer had no problem explaining them to the participants and the viewers. He stayed with the show, taking on another hosting job for Goodson and Todman in 1956 with *To Tell The Truth*. His tenure on that show lasted for twelve years on CBS.

Bud Collyer died of heart failure at age 61 in September of 1969.

NAME: Bill Cullen (William Lawrence Cullen)

BIRTHDATE: February 20, 1920

DATE OF DEATH: July 7, 1990

BIRTHPLACE: Pittsburgh, Pennsylvania

MAJOR GAME SHOWS: *Name That Tune* (1954 - 1955), *The Price Is Right* (1956 – 1965), *The $25,000 Pyramid* (1974 – 1979), *Blockbusters* (1980 – 1982), *Joker's Wild* (1984 – 1986)

Memorials from his peers earned Bill Cullen kudos like "class," "great intelligence," and "a broadcaster's broadcaster" when he died of lung cancer in 1990. Any man stricken with the debilitating disease of polio and wearing thick glasses may hardly be the icon of TV game shows, but Cullen was no ordinary man.

A pre-med student at the University of Pittsburgh, Cullen ran out of funds and looked into the world of radio announcing. He soon had enough to return to school, but traded in a scalpel for a microphone and earned a degree in fine arts. He soon began hosting radio shows and made the acquaintance of Mark Goodson and Bill Todman.

By the 1950s, Cullen was a panelist on *I've Got A Secret* and hosting *The Price Is Right*. The need for his services never faded – most accounts credit him with hosting a record twenty-three TV game shows across a career that spanned nearly fifty years.

NAME: Bob Eubanks (Robert Leland Eubanks)

BIRTHDATE: January 8, 1938

BIRTHPLACE: Flint, Michigan

MAJOR GAME SHOWS: *Newlywed Game* (1966 – 1974, 1977 – 1980, 1997 - 1999), *Trivia Trap* (1984 - 1985), *The New Newlywed Game* (1985 – 1988), *Card Sharks* (1986 – 1989)

A cowboy at heart, Bob Eubanks was a major personality in Top 40 radio and concert promotion in Southern California long before he took the podium for *The Newlywed Game*. Among his early promotional triumphs was bringing the Beatles to the Hollywood Bowl for their landmark 1964 concert.

Producer Chuck Barris tapped Eubanks for *The Newlywed Game* in 1966 and the host stayed (with few gaps) through the 60s, 70s, 80s and 90s. During the same time, Eubanks managed the country music careers of Dolly Parton and Barbara Mandrell, among others. During the trivia craze of the mid-1980s, he hosted *Trivia Trap* and, later, *Card Sharks*.

Eubanks now spends his time as a corporate speaker – when he's not riding horses and roping steers on his California cattle ranch.

NAME:	Monty Hall (Monte Halperin)
BIRTHDATE:	August 25, 1921
BIRTHPLACE:	Winnipeg, Manitoba, Canada
MAJOR GAME SHOWS:	*Twenty-One* (1958), *Video Village* (1960 - 1962), *Let's Make A Deal* (1963 – 1977, 1980 – 1981, 1990 – 1991, 2003), *All New Let's Make A Deal* (1984 – 1986)

Like many TV game show hosts, Canadian-born Monty Hall has a diverse resume, but will always be identified by one show – *Let's Make A Deal*. His association with the trading game covers five decades.

Degreed in chemistry from the University of Manitoba, Hall spent more than ten years in Canadian radio, including hosting talk and quiz shows. His first major TV quiz show was *Bingo-At-Home* for a New York City station in 1958. By 1963, he had formed a production company with Stefan Hatos and created *Let's Make A Deal* for NBC. Ratings soared and Hall became the "Master Dealmaker."

Hall has also spent much of his life on philanthropic projects, helping to raise nearly $1 billion dollars for Variety Clubs International.

NAME: Dennis James (Demie James Sposa)

BIRTHDATE: August 24, 1917

DATE OF DEATH: June 3, 1997

BIRTHPLACE: Jersey City, New Jersey

MAJOR GAME SHOWS: *Name's The Same* (1954 - 1955), *PDQ* (1965 – 1969), *The Price Is Right* (1972 – 1977), *Name That Tune* (1974 – 1975)

A true television pioneer, Dennis James is noted by many sources as TV's first game show host, appearing on the DuMont network show, *Cash and Carry*, in 1946. In a career that spanned seven decades, James left his mark on many game shows.

He hosted *The Name's The Same* for ABC in the mid-1950s and was a longtime spokesperson for many commercial products. James led the syndicated *PDQ* for four seasons and became the primetime host for *The Price Is Right* in 1972. He also helmed the revival of *Name That Tune* in the mid-1970s.

Dennis James also gave generously of his time and money to benefits like United Cerebral Palsy and Childhelp International, hosting telethons for nearly thirty years. He died from lung cancer in 1997.

NAME: Tom Kennedy (James Edward Narz)

BIRTHDATE: February 26, 1927

BIRTHPLACE: Louisville, Kentucky

MAJOR GAME SHOWS: *You Don't Say!* (1963 – 1969, 1975), *Split Second* (1965 – 1969), *$100,000 Name That Tune* (1974 – 1981), *Password Plus* (1980 – 1982), *The Price Is Right* (1985 – 1986)

As a younger brother, it's always tough living under the shadow of an older sibling. For Jim Narz, it was a blessing. When older brother Jack Narz enrolled in a California radio school, Jim followed suit. Both found themselves in radio by the end of the 1940s.

Jim Narz changed his professional name to Tom Kennedy when he became the spokesperson for Plymouth cars in 1957, since his brother Jack was already known in the broadcasting world. Kennedy's first game show was *Big Game* on NBC, but he really struck gold with *You Don't Say!* in 1963. He continued with *Split Second*, *The $100,000 Name That Tune, Password Plus*, and *The Price Is Right,* totaling fifteen major game shows in his career.

Kennedy retired in the mid-1990s to his home in California.

NAME:	Allen Ludden (Allen Packard Ellsworth)
BIRTHDATE:	October 5, 1917
DATE OF DEATH:	June 9, 1981
BIRTHPLACE:	Mineral Point, Wisconsin
MAJOR GAME SHOWS:	*College Bowl* (1959 - 1962), *Password* (1961 – 1967, 1971 - 1975), *Password Plus* (1979 – 1980)

Holding a master's degree in English, Allen Ludden brought a high-class, controlled approach to game show hosting. His TV tenure for more than twenty years brought stability to a format that had suffered under the game show scandals.

Like many hosts, Ludden began his work in radio, helping to create and host NBC's *College Bowl* in 1953. When the show moved to TV in 1959, so did Ludden. He picked up the hosting chores for *Password* in 1961, where he made the acquaintance of guest celebrity Betty White. The couple married in 1963.

Ludden often began his shows with the greeting, "Hi, Doll." Speculation for years suggested he had a life-sized mannequin propped up at this house in front of the TV – so that Ludden was always assured of having someone (or something) watching his performance. The more logical explanation is that he was sending best regards to Betty White's mom, a loyal viewer.

Ludden succumbed to stomach cancer in 1981, leaving widow Betty White to continue making daytime and primetime TV appearances.

NAME: Peter Marshall (Ralph Pierre LaCock)

BIRTHDATE: March 30, 1927

BIRTHPLACE: Clarksburg, West Virginia

MAJOR GAME SHOWS: *Hollywood Squares* (1966 – 1981)

Peter Marshall's diverse early experiences as a singer, radio disc jockey, and comedy team straight man laid the foundation for his "zookeeper" role as host of *Hollywood Squares* for fifteen years.

While Marshall made appearances as a guest on episodic television, as well as nightclubs and Broadway, he remained closely associated with *Hollywood Squares*. In his autobiography, Marshall claimed he took the hosting role, partly because rival comic Dan Rowan was in line for the position, saying he wanted to, "screw Dan Rowan out of a job."

Marshall's easy-going style and experience as a comic straight man made him a perfect match for the nine celebrities seated in the grid. Yet, he tired of the show in the mid-70s and yearned to move on to other projects. Every time he asked for a raise (figuring producers would deny his request and let him go,) he received the increase he requested.

Yet, Marshall remains proud of his work and the success of *Hollywood Squares*.

NAME:	Wink Martindale (Winston Conrad Martindale)
BIRTHDATE:	December 4, 1933
BIRTHPLACE:	Jackson, Tennessee
MAJOR GAME SHOWS:	*Gambit* (1972 – 1976), *Tic Tac Dough* (1978 – 1985), *High Rollers* (1987 – 1988), *Trivial Pursuit* (1993 – 1995)

With a nickname of "Wink," bestowed by a boyhood pal in Jackson, Tennessee, Winston Martindale was into spinning records on the radio, even before graduating high school. In a broadcasting career that lasted nearly fifty years, Martindale was second only to Bill Cullen in number of game shows hosted – nineteen.

He landed his first major game show in 1972 with *Gambit*, which lasted for five seasons on CBS. Wink followed up with a long run in *Tic Tac Dough*, again on CBS, as well as syndication. Martindale developed some of the first real-time interactive game shows, including *Trivial Pursuit, Boggle*, and *Shuffle*, for the Family Channel cable network in the mid-1990s.

Hardly a one-trick pony, Wink Martindale had a Billboard Top 10 record in 1959 (called, "Deck of Cards",) owned a restaurant for several years in the 1980s, and wrote his autobiography – *Winking At Life* – in 2000.

NAME: Jack Narz (John L. Narz, Jr.)

BIRTHDATE: November 13, 1922

DATE OF DEATH: October 15, 2008

BIRTHPLACE: Louisville, Kentucky

MAJOR GAME SHOWS: *Dotto* (1958), *Video Village* (1960), *Seven Keys* (1961 – 1964), *Beat The Clock* (1969 – 1972), *Concentration* (1973 – 1978)

Growing up a boy who loved flying, Jack Narz found himself as a flight instructor after World War II. While attending a radio announcing school, Narz landed jobs as a radio and TV announcer in the late 1940s and into the 50s.

Hosting the game show *Dotto* in 1958 almost doomed his career, as it became the first show revealed to be rigged and cancelled in the game show scandals. But Narz had no knowledge at all concerning the rigging and survived, hosting *Top Dollar* a few months later.

He continued into the 1960s, hosting *Video Village* for CBS, *Seven Keys* for ABC, and the syndicated *Beat The Clock*. Most of the 70s were spent helming *Concentration* for syndication.

Weary of the business, Jack Narz retired in the early 1980s, concentrating on traveling with his wife and playing golf. He passed away in 2008.

NAME: Regis Philbin (Regis Francis Xavier Philbin)

BIRTHDATE: August 25, 1931

BIRTHPLACE: New York, New York

MAJOR GAME SHOWS: *Who Wants To Be A Millionaire* (1999 - 2004), *Million Dollar Password* (2008)

A friendly, "everyman" kind of TV personality, Regis Philbin was not known as a game show host before 1999. The unprecedented success of *Who Wants To Be A Millionaire* allowed Philbin to single-handedly put the catch-phrase – "Is that your final answer?" on the lips of millions of viewers every week.

A graduate of the University of Notre Dame with a degree in sociology, Philbin entered the broadcasting industry as a writer and stagehand for a Los Angeles TV station. Moving to San Diego, he became a news anchor and local talk show host. By the late 1960s, he was the on-camera sidekick for Joey Bishop's ABC late night show. He continued through the next three decades as a national talk show host and personality, including co-hosting a live weekday show from New York with Kathy Lee Gifford and, currently, Kelly Ripa.

As the host of *Who Wants To Be A Millionaire,* Philbin guided contestants through the questions and answers that could lead to $1 million. His success as a game show host resulted in his role on CBS's *Million Dollar Password* in 2008.

NAME: Gene Rayburn (Eugene Rubessa)

BIRTHDATE: December 22, 1917

DATE OF DEATH: November 29, 1999

BIRTHPLACE: Christopher, Illinois

MAJOR GAME SHOWS: *Tic Tac Dough* (1956 - 1957), *Dough Re Mi* (1958 - 1960), *Play Your Hunch* (1962), *Match Game* (1962 – 1969, 1973 – 1982), *Match Game – Hollywood Squares Hour* (1983 – 1984)

Gene Rayburn's lasting legacy is a combination of radio, television and theater highlights that few other entertainers have enjoyed. In a career that lasted more than thirty years, he worked on ground-breaking shows and left his own brand of wit and humor with them.

A bonafide radio personality in the 1940s, Rayburn hosted a morning show with Jack Lescoulie on WNEW in New York City, becoming the first two-person morning team in radio. By the mid-1950s, he was the announcer/sidekick for Steve Allen on NBC-TV's *Tonight Show*.

Rayburn started his game show chores with *Tic Tac Dough* and *Dough Re Mi* in the 50s. He took over for Merv Griffin on *Play Your Hunch* in 1962. But his biggest chance to show his skills came with *The Match Game*, starting in 1962 and ending more than twenty years later with *The Match Game – Hollywood Squares Hour.*

Rayburn died in 1999, having received a Lifetime Achievement Award from the National Academy of Television Arts and Sciences one month earlier.

(As a favor to the author and publisher in the mid-1990s, Gene Rayburn narrate the video/DVD companion to this book, *TV's Greatest Game Shows*.)

NAME: Pat Sajak (Patrick Leonard Sajak)

BIRTHDATE: October 26, 1946

BIRTHPLACE: Chicago, Illinois

MAJOR GAME SHOWS: *Wheel Of Fortune* (1981 - present)

Pat Sajak's silly but low-key personality has taken him through the worlds of radio, television news, talk shows – and one game show that has kept him busy for more than twenty-five years.

Hailing from Chicago, Sajak spent some time at Columbia College, a performing arts school, but left when a chance to be a newsreader at a local radio station came up. Following disc jockey stints in Armed Forces Radio (in Vietnam) and Nashville, he moved to KNBC-TV in Los Angeles as a weatherman in 1977.

Merv Griffin noticed Sajak and placed him as the new host of *Wheel Of Fortune* in 1981, replacing Chuck Woolery. With Vanna White turning letters, Sajak has presided over the show ever since.

NAME: Alex Trebek (George Alexander Trebek)

BIRTHDATE: July 22, 1940

BIRTHPLACE: Sudbury, Ontario, Canada

MAJOR GAME SHOWS: *Wizard Of Odds* (1973 - 1974), *High Rollers* (1974 - 1976), *The New High Rollers* (1978 – 1980), *Battlestars* (1981 – 1982), *Jeopardy!* (1984 – present), *Classic Concentration* (1987 – 1990)

Like Monty Hall, Alex Trebek is a native of Canada. In fact, Trebek had a long and successful career in Canadian television, hosting news and music programs, as well as game shows, before breaking into the American market in 1973.

Graduating from the University of Ottawa with a degree in philosophy, Trebek had paid his way by announcing with a Canadian radio station. His career in broadcasting was a natural extension, leading to a major role on the Canadian Broadcasting Corporation – CBC.

Once in the USA, Trebek established his aloof, intellectual persona as host of the *Wizard of Odds* on NBC, then *High Rollers* and *Double Dare*. He continued with *Battlestars* and *Classic Concentration*, but scored big as host of the new *Jeopardy!* that hit the air in 1984. Twenty-five years later, Trebek and the show are still going strong.

NAME: Chuck Wollery (Charles Herbert Wollery)

BIRTHDATE: March 16, 1941

BIRTHPLACE: Ashland, Kentucky

MAJOR GAME SHOWS: *Wheel Of Fortune* (1975 - 1981), *Love Connection* (1983 – 1994), *Scrabble* (1984 – 1990, 1993), *Dating Game* (1997 – 1999), *Greed* (1999 – 2000) *Lingo* (2002 – 2008)

Chuck Woolery started his public life with an eye on being a country music star. While he did land a hit single in Nashville, it was his first AND last hit. After a brief try at acting in Los Angeles, Woolery got an offer from Merv Griffin to host a new game show.

Even though Woolery was not exactly thrilled at the prospect, he took the job – and became host of *Wheel of Fortune* in 1975. A salary dispute ended his association with the show in 1981, but Woolery picked up *Love Connection* in 1983, hosting for eleven years.

He continued with shows like *Scrabble, the Dating Game*, and *Greed* (during the game show craze created by *Millionaire*.) Woolery later landed a steady hosting gig on the Game Show Network program, *Lingo*.

Through good times and bad, Woolery's Christian faith has kept him positive and on top of the game show mountain.

GAME SHOWS OF TODAY

Game Shows of Today

TV game shows have come and gone for nearly sixty years, with the line between them and reality shows becoming blurred. Is *American Idol* a game show? Is *Deal or No Deal* a reality show? Which is more embarrassing – watching a man trying to put on a girdle in *Truth or Consequences* from the 1950s, or watching an adult trying to answer grade-school questions on *Are You Smarter Than A 5th Grader* from today?

Most likely, the answers are immaterial – they're all entertainment. There's no question that today's TV game shows are edgier than their forefathers, packed with high-energy audio and video technology. For the most part, money and prizes won on today's shows are bigger, with higher values than yesterday's shows. But are they BETTER? Not likely, as knock-offs and imitations hardly ever top the originals.

Here are some of today's offerings.

Are You Smarter Than A 5thGrader?

February 7, 2007 (2 seasons)

Network: FOX

Host(s): Jeff Foxworthy

Creator(s): Mark Burnett

Producer(s): Benjamin Silverman

Director(s): Debbie Palacios, Don Weiner

Jeff Foxworthy & 5th Graders

Hosted by cornpone comedian Jeff Foxworthy, *Are You Smarter Than A 5th Grader* asks adults questions from grade-school textbooks. Top winners can take home up to $1 million – as long as they beat out the fifth graders.

<u>Deal or No Deal</u>

Howie Mandel & Briefcase Girls

December 19, 2005 (3 seasons)

Network:	NBC primetime (Syndicated daytme– September 8, 2008)
Host(s):	Howie Mandel
Creator(s):	Dick Derijk
Producer(s):	Scott St. John, Mashawn Nix
Director(s):	Alan Carter

It doesn't get much simpler than *Deal or No Deal* – Contestants challenge the odds to select a $1 million briefcase from 26 possibilities. As contestants eliminate briefcases, they are tempted to accept a sure deal from an unknown "Banker."

<u>Greatest American Dog</u>

July 10, 2008 (1 season)

Network:	CBS primetime
Host(s):	Jarod Miller
Creator(s):	R.J. Cutler

Producer(s): R.J. Cutler

Director(s): NA

Jarod Miller & co-star

Twelve teams of owners and dogs compete for the title of Top Dog and a cash prize of $250,000. Every week, they perform various stunts, tricks, and talents, with one team sent home at the end of the show.

Hurl!

July 15, 2008 (1 season)

Network: G4 cable channel

Host(s): None

Creator(s): Tom Crehan, Dale Roy Robinson

Producer(s): Tom Crehan, Dale Roy Robinson

Director(s): NA

A show of this sort seemed inevitable – contestants eat, drink, and then are abused until they (program title here.) The last one to (program title here) or not (program title here) at all wins $1,000.

Hurl! contestants

Lingo

August 5, 2002 – 2008 (6 seasons)

Network: Game Show Network

Host(s): Chuck Woolery

Creator(s): Ralph Edwards

Producer(s): Harry de Winter, Philip Gurin, Marc Jansen

Director(s): R. Brian DiPirro, Dirk-Jan Van Heusden, John Vogt

Shandi Finnessey & Chuck Woolery

Lingo was a word-guessing game combined with Bingo-type balls, played by two teams of two players each. With Chuck Woolery at the helm, winners received vacation trips and cash.

Wipeout

June 24, 2008 (1 season)

Network: ABC primetime

Host(s): John Anderson, John Henson, Jill Wagner

Creator(s): Matt Kunitz

Producer(s): Trice Barto

Director(s): J. Rupert Thompson

Contestants try to avoid elimination by conquering various and silly obstacle courses with funny names. *Wipeout* owes its roots to the Japanese game show *Takeshi's Castle* (and the subsequent English-dubbed comedy on Spike TV, *MXC*.)

Wipeout **contestant**

TV's Greatest GAME SHOWS Timeline

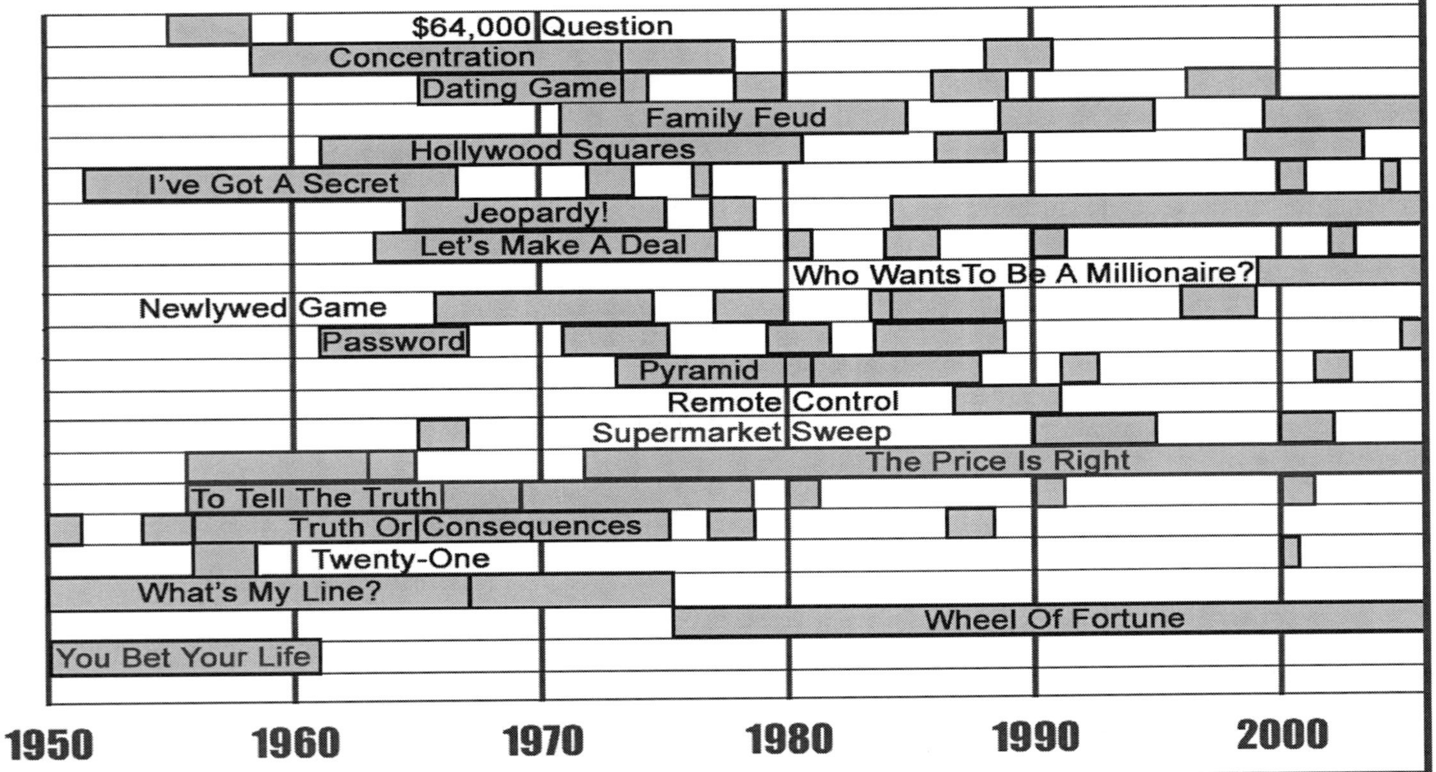

Index

GAME SHOW INDEX

PEOPLE INDEX